M000100256

U.S. Stocks Even High School Students Can Understand

高校生にも分かる米国株

Finance with Hanako

Published by Japanese with Hanako

http://www.financewithhanako.com

目次

INDEX

はじめに
Introduction

皆さんこんにちは、花子です！
Hi everyone, I'm Hanako!

「高校生にも分かる米国株」によう
こそ！
Welcome to "U.S. Stocks Even
High School Students Can
Understand"!

私は、日本生まれ、日本育ちで大学
は日本文学専攻です。
I was born and raised in Japan,
and I majored in Japanese
literature at a university in my
home country.

しかし、私はアメリカのカレッジで会計を勉強して、アメリカに
ある日本の銀行で15年働きました。
Later, I ended up studying accounting at a college in
America, and worked for 15 years at a Japanese Bank in
that country.

私は日本語を教えるのが楽しいから教えているのですが、それ
以外にも何か楽しいことをしたいな〜と考えていました。
I teach Japanese because I enjoy doing it, though, I was
thinking I want to do something fun other than teaching
Japanese.

そこで、「あ、そうだ。米国株入門という本を書こう！」と思いつきました。
Then I thought, "Oh, I want to write about American stocks for beginner investors!"

私は子供の頃から文章を書くのが好きでした。
I've always liked writing since I was a child.

１５年間クレジットアナリストをしてきたので、株を買うのが好きです。
I enjoy buying stocks since I was a credit analyst for the past 15 years.

１５年間毎日毎日会社の決算書を見てきたのに、去年脱サラして銀行を辞めて以来、決算書を見るのは株を買うときだけになりました。
Although I had been reading corporate financial statements every day for15 years, I still look at financial statements only when I buy stocks since quitting my full-time job.

そうなると、決算書を読みたくなってきます。
Now, I want to read financial statements.

日本人は株を買うことに慣れていません。
Japanese people are not too familiar with buying stocks.

アメリカでも日常的ではないにしても、会社に入れば４０１Ｋがありますし、政府が行なっているIRAなどもありますよね。
It's probably not a part of daily life for the average American to buy stocks, though when they work, many companies will provide 401K and the government will provide IRA for people who don't have full-time jobs.

日本では国民年金、厚生年金にお金を払いますが、株ではありませんし、少子化が進んでいる現在、年金は本当にもらえるのか疑って払っていない人も多いです。
In Japan, we pay for a national pension and employee pension plan, but it's not stock. As the number of children is decreasing, many people do not pay for those.

会社で正社員の場合は給料から引かれますが、それ以外の人は年金を払わないということもできます。ただし、将来の受取額は減ります。
If you work for companies as a full-time employee, the money for the employee pension plan will be deducted from your salary. Other than that, it's not always necessary to pay for national pension although those who do not will receive less money when they retire.

アメリカ経済は世界一ですから、日本の株はアメリカの影響を受けて上がったり下がったりしますが、アメリカ株はやっぱり日本株よりも強いのです。
The U.S. economy is the best in the world, so Japanese stocks will fluctuate in accordance with U.S. stocks, but U.S. stocks are definitely stronger than their Japanese counterparts.

なぜ英語訳が付いているのか、と言うと、最終的には自分で英語の決算書を読めるようになって欲しいからです。
The reason why I added English translation is because eventually, I would like you to be able to read financial statements written in English.

自分の頭で考えることが大切です。そのためには自分で英語の
決算書を読む必要があります。
It's important to be able to evaluate U.S. stocks by
yourself. In order to do that, it's necessary to be able to
read financial statements in English.

ということで、この本を書きました!
So, I wrote this book!

鈴木　花子
Hanako Suzuki

オンラインレッスンの情報はこちら:
http://www.financewithhanako.com/class/

第1章 - 高校生にも分かる米国株
CH1 - U.S. Stocks Even High School Students Can Understand

アメリカから去年(2018年)日本に帰ってきました。
I moved back to Japan from America last year (2018).

クレジットアナリストをアメリカで15年してきましたが、今は脱サラしてオンラインでなぜか日本語を教えています。
Although I had been working as a credit analyst in the past 15 years in America, I quit my full-time job to teach Japanese online for some reason.

決算書を読まなくなって数ヶ月、決算書が恋しくなりました。
I didn't need to read financial statements for months and I started to miss it.

日本の株も買ってみようかと楽天証券の口座を開けましたが、いろいろ調べた結果全く買う気にはなりませんでした。
Although I opened an investment account with Rakuten Investment Company, I did not want to buy Japanese stocks after reviewing them.

理由は色々ありますが、いくらその日本の会社の決算結果が良くても、アメリカの会社のようには株価が上がっていないのです。
There are several reasons, one of them being that the price of Japanese stocks do not rise as much as American stocks do.

アメリカ経済は世界第一位ですから、やはり国の力というもの
は大きいですね。
Since the American economy ranks No.1 in the world, I
can't deny that its economic strength is huge.

また、アメリカ株は一株から買えるので、＄１０の株を買って、
手数料が＄７くらいで合計２０ドル以下でも買えます。
Also, you can buy an American stock starting from one
unit, so let's say if you buy a stock for $10, you pay a $7
fee and it comes to less than $20.

しかし日本の場合、単独株を買う場合には、100株まとめて買
わないといけないので、ユニクロの株を買うのに現在は67,000
円なので、その100倍、670万円からしか買えないんです。アメ
リカドルだと約67,000ドルですよ（1ドル＝100円/2019年12
月17日現在）。
However, if you buy Japanese stock, you have to buy
them in bundles of 100, so if you want to buy Uniqlo
stock, one stock is 67,000 yen, so your starting budget
will have to be 670,000 yen. That's about US$67,000
(100yen/$, as of 12/17/2019).

初めて株を買う人が、こんなに払えないですよね。
A beginner investor can't pay this much, right?

ということで、私の株はすべて米国株です。
So, all my stocks are U.S. stocks.

米国株で一番安全なのは、mutual fund （またはETF）という
500インデックスファンドのようなもので、私の株のほとんど
はそのmutual fund （株のまとまり）です。
The least risky investment in the U.S. is the mutual fund
(or ETF) which is a collection of U.S. stocks such as S&P

500 index fund, and in Japan they're called index stocks, or toshi-shintaku.

去年は、アップル株が一番下がった2018年年末年始、142ドルの時に買いました。2019年の12月現在は280ドル近くになっています。
Last year I purchased Apple stock when prices plunged to $142. Currently (as of 12/2019, it's around $280.)

株がどんどん下がっている時期で、5兆円のアップル株を持っているウォーレンバフェットは叩かれていましたね。
When the US stocks were declining, many analysts criticized Warren Buffet who held around $50 billion in Apple stock.

2018年12月には株価が下がっていくネットフレックス株を1株230ドルで買って、今2019年12月の時点で1株304ドルくらいまで上がっています。
In Dec 2018, when the stock price of Netflix plunged, I bought some for $230 per stock, and now it's risen to $304 per stock.

もうちょっとこれから高校生でもわかるような説明をしていこうかなあと思っています。
I would like to explain in more detail about it in a way even high school students can understand.

第2章 - 私が米国アナリストになったわけ
CH2 - The Reason Why I Became an Analyst in America

私は実は日本文学科卒業です。
I actually majored in Japanese literature.

アメリカでクレジットアナリストを15年間しました。
I had been working as a credit analyst for the past 15 years in America.

アメリカにある日本の銀行２社でも働きました。
I have also worked at two Japanese banks in America.

日本だったら私の大学で、日本文学卒業なんて言ったら、クレジットアナリストとして採用しないでしょうね。
In Japan, Japanese banks would not hire me as a credit analyst because I majored in Japanese literature.

私のキャリアを説明すると、こうです。
My career path went like this.

大学を卒業した後、食品会社に就職しましたが満員電車と残業が嫌で半年でやめる。（ダメ人間っぽい）
After I graduated from University, I was hired by a food company, however, I ended up quitting after 6 months because I hated the crowded train and the overtime (sounds like a useless person).

その後、１年間オーストラリアワーホリに行く（ありがち）。
Later, I lived in Australia with a working visa (typical).

1年いても、英語は全く話せない。（結構知られていないが、ありがち）
Although I had been there for a year, my English did not improve at all (Japanese people don't know this, but it's typical).

そこで免税店の経理部で働くが、給料安いし、シドニーの家賃は高いしで、貧乏な生活を経験し、「海外に住むなら、やっぱ駐在員っしょ！」と決めて帰国（ダメ人間が考えそうなこと）。
There I worked at the accountant's division of a duty free shop, however, the salary was low and the rent in Sydney was expensive, so I experienced a poor life. Then I thought, "If I live overseas, I should be a resident employee of a Japanese company!", and returned to Japan (seems like something a failure might think).

とらばーゆを見て（求人情報雑誌）「海外勤務できます！」という文字に引かれて、大手英会話学校のマネージャーになりました。
I saw a job opening in Toravayu (a job hunting magazine), and saw the words, "Working overseas is possible!", so then I became a school manager at a major ESL (English as a second language) school.

入ってみると、地獄のようなセールス目標半端なく、達成できないと精神的に追い詰められました。
After I joined that company, I realized how high the sales targets were, and when we couldn't reach that goal, we were blamed until we felt very depressed.

１３人同期で入ったけれど、気がつくと残ったのは私だけでした。

Thirteen new employees were hired including me, but I later realized that I was only one who remained at that company.

まさにブラック企業。。。
(日本ではブラック企業は労働法に違反することをしている、または、ギリギリなことをしている会社という意味です)

It's really a so-called "black company".
（＊A black company means it does not follow labor low or is almost doing something illegal.)

ダメ人間的な甘い思考を持ちつつも、結構淡々と仕事をこなし、全国５００人くらいいたスクールマネージャーの中でもトップ１０に常に入る。

While having a loser's mindset, I achieved tasks one by one, and my sales result always ranked top 10 out of 500 school managers in Japan.

それもこれも、海外勤務で駐在員として金に苦労のない生活を送るためだった。

I could make the effort to achieve my goal of living a comfortable life as an overseas residential employee.

そして、２、3年でカナダ、バンクーバー駐在決定。

A few years later, I was assigned to work at the Company's Vancouver branch in Canada.

ダメ人間思考なのに、意外と達成した。

I had thought my way of thinking sounded like that of a loser, however I was able to succeed.

住んだ家は、まさに当時３億円の会社が保有する豪邸で、シルベスタースターローンなどがご近所さんだった。
The house I lived in was a mansion that the company owned and was valued about $3 million at the time. My neighbors included famous actors such as Sylvester Stallone

車はトヨタだったが、いちおうセレブ的な生活を送る、かのように見えた。
My car was Toyota, but it really looked like the celebrity lifestyle… or so I thought.
しかし、セールスの高い目標設定と、日本から来た生徒たちの世話で、フラフラになる。
However, I was too exhausted from high sales targets and busy life to take care of my students from Japan.

海外に来た日本人の若い生徒たちは、やりたい放題。ホームステイ先からの苦情処理もあり。。。
Some young Japanese students who came overseas for the first time had gone wild. I often received complaints from their homestay families.

私だって、やりたい放題したい２０代なのに！と思いました。
I thought, "I am also a young girl in her 20's who wants to be wild!".

毎日泣きながら仕事。
I worked every day with the occasional crying.

先生たちは全員カナダ人だったが、採用活動までしないといけない。
All the teachers were Canadian, and I had to do hiring jobs as well.

そして、まだ２０代だというのに、アメリカの会社で働く父が、私が結婚しないことを心配して、なぜかカナダに日系アメリカ人男性を連れてきて、お見合いのようなブラインドデート？

Then, although I was in my 20's, my father who worked at an American company worried about me, and for some reason he brought a Japanese-American man to set me up on a blind date with.

で、結婚して、アメリカに引っ越しました。

And we got married and moved to America.

結婚してすぐに娘がお腹の中にいました。

Right after we got married, my daughter was in my tummy.

妊娠しても、働くのは当たり前、と元旦那さんに言われ、というか、旦那さんのお兄さんが言っていたそうですが、

My ex-husband told me it's natural that pregnant woman have a job. Actually, maybe his older brother said that.

つわり真っ只中で、見知らぬ土地アメリカで就職活動スタート。。。

I started job hunting while I had morning sickness in the new frontier, America.

日本人に言うとびっくりされますが、アメリカ人に言うと妊娠してることを言わずに面接を受けたことを「普通じゃない？」と言われます。

When I talk about this with Japanese people, they get surprised, however, many Americans say, "It's not so surprising that a pregnant woman would do job hunting without telling the interviewer that she is pregnant."

最初は、電話会社で働いていて、銀行ではなかったんですが、いや〜大変だった。
At first, I worked at a telecommunications company. It was actually really tough.

旦那さんは、残業の少ないのが一般的なアメリカなのに、毎日１０時から１２時に帰ってきていました。保育園の娘のお迎えは毎日私だったので、仕事、料理、洗濯などで忙しかったです。
My ex-husband came home around 10pm to 12am although overtime is not so common in America. I also had to pick up my daughter from daycare, so I was super busy with my full-time job, cooking, laundry, and so on.

その後、その会社が引っ越して保育園のお迎えが間に合わなくなったので、たまたま募集していた日本の銀行のアシスタントに受かりました。
Later, the company was relocated and I was unable to pick up my daughter from daycare on time, so I found a different job in an assistant position at the Japanese bank by chance.

そこでアシスタントの仕事をしているうちに、このままじゃ給料上がらないな、と思い、米国公認会計士のテストを受けることができるくらいの会計の単位を取ろうと思いました。
While I worked as an assistant, I thought it was difficult to increase my salary, so I decided to take accounting classes in order to take the U.S. CPA exam.

しかし、子供も小さいし、フルタイムで働き旦那さんの手伝い
は一切なかったので、学校に行くのは無理でした。
On the top of that, it was difficult to go to on-sight school
without my ex-husband's help because my daughter was
so small and I had a full-time job.

また、お母さんに学費を払ってくれる家庭ってなかなかないです
よね。
Also it's quite rare that a family pay expensive tuition for
the mother.

そこで、サンタモニカカレッジというコミュニティカレッジで
オンラインクラスを取ることにしました。
So I decided to take online classes at a community
college called Santa Monica College.

コミュニティーカレッジというのは、日本でいう短大みたいな
ものですが、会計の単位はCPAテストを受けるための単位にカ
ウントできるし、大学よりもかなり安いです。
Community college is similar to a two-year college
equivalent or an AA or AS degree. The credits you take
will be counted to sit for the CPA exam and the tuition is
much cheaper than four-year university.

私の場合は一単位が当時20ドルくらいでしたが、それはカリフ
ォルニア州に1年以上住んでいたからです。
I paid $20 per credit since I lived in California more than
a year with a resident visa.

留学生は1単位300ドルくらいだと思います。
For international students, one credit would be about
$300.

カリフォルニアで米国会計士のテストを受けるには、4年生大学卒業と、会計と経済の科目４８単位が必要なので、留学生だったら125万円学費という感じでしょうか。（州により違う）。
In order to be eligible to sit for the U.S. CPA exam, you are required to have a bachelor's degree and 48 credits of accounting and business classes in California (this varies per state).

でも、アメリカの州立大学、例えばUCLAは一年の学費が150万円、留学生だと300万円です。私立大学は１年間に500万円かかりますから、コミュニティカレッジはそれほど悪くはないです。
However, the tuition of public schools, such as UCLA, is $15,000 for resident and $30,000 for international students.

日本の大学を出て、アメリカのコミュニティカレッジで単位をとる、というのもいいと思います。
It's also worth it to consider taking classes at community college after you graduate from university in Japan.

私の場合は、コミュニティカレッジで公認会計士を受けるために必要な単位も取れたので、テストを受け始めました。
In my case, I started taking the CPA exam since I completed classes to sit for the exam.

銀行ではアシスタントをしていましたが、カレッジで単位を取ったことを言うと、クレジットアナリストにしてくれました。
I had been an assistant at a bank. When I told my boss that I took classes at community college, they gave me the position of credit analyst.

そして、テストを受けている途中に大手の銀行に2倍くらい給料アップで転職できたので、忙しいしテストを受けるのを辞めてしまいました。

Then, while I was taking the CPA exam, I was accepted by a larger sized bank and my salary was doubled, so I stopped taking the exam since I was busy with my new position.

実際、経験さえあればテストに受かっているいるかどうかは関係ないようでした。

Actually, if we already have experience as a credit analyst, it does not matter if we passed the CPA exam or not.

ライセンスにするためには、会計事務所で働かないといけません。

If you want to get a CPA license, you have to work at an accounting firm.

会計事務所での経験がない場合、公認会計士のテストに受かっていると言うのはいいですが、銀行で働いてもライセンスにはならないのでまあいいかと辞めました。

If you haven't worked at an accounting firm, even if you passed the CPA exam, you can't claim you are a CPA but you can say you passed the exam. The experience working at the bank can't be counted, so I quit taking exam.

こう言う経緯を踏んでクレジットアナリストとなりましたが、元々は日本文学科卒業です。

This is how I became a credit analyst. Originally I majored in Japanese literature.

第3章 - 長期投資が本物の金持ちになる
CH3 - Long-Term Investment Makes You A Real Wealthy Person

私は去年までアメリカにある日本の銀行で１５年間クレジットアナリストをしていたので、普通よりは株に詳しいです。
I had been working at a Japanese bank in America for the past 15 years, so I know more about stock investments than the average person.

私は株で損したことはありませんが、買う株は全て米国株です。理由はアメリカが世界一の経済力があるからです。
I've never lost money in investments, though I only buy U.S. stocks. That's because the American economy is the best in the world.

過去の米国株の上がり方が良かったのもあります。
There's also the fact that U.S. stock has soared in the past.

本物の金持ちは、ただ置いとくだけで自然にお金が増えていく長期投資がほとんどです。
Most wealthy people in America invest in the long-term where they just leave money in and it grows and grows.

正直、株が大好きで、絶対これは成長株、と思って買うので、売る意味が分かりません。
To be honest, I don't know why people would sell their stocks because I only buy stocks which I believe are going to do very well in the future.

ほっとけばどんどん上がります。
If you leave it alone, it will only go up.

本当は、株の集まりのmutual fund やETFが一番安全です。
Actually, the safest investment is a "mutual fund" or
"ETF", a collection of stocks.

その次に安全なのは、昔からあるコカコーラとかマクドナルド
とか、普段あまり株の動きが小さいけど、地味一に上がってい
く株です。
The next safest ones to invest in are major companies
that have been around a very long time such as Coca-
Cola or McDonald's

長い歴史のある安定した会社は、配当することが多いですが、
アマゾンとかグーグルなどの成長企業は配当金はあまり出しま
せん。
Stable companies with long histories often declare
dividends, however, rapidly growing companies like
Amazon or Google rarely pay out dividends.

配当金とは、例えばあなたがマクドナルドの株、220ドルを10
株、合計2,200ドル持っているとします。
As for dividend payout, let's say you have 10 $220
stocks of McDonald's, amounting to $2200.

配当利回りは上のように、2.11%と書いてあるので、1年に持っ
ている株、2,200ドルの2.11%、つまり46.4ドルもらえます。
Dividend yield is stated to be 2.11% as pictured above, so
you will get $46.4, 2.11% of $2,200 a year.

そして次に安全なのは、「手作りミューチュアルファンド」、私が作った言葉です。
The next safest option is a "handmade mutual fund", a term I just came up with myself.

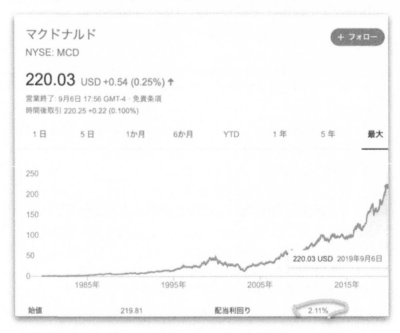

自分で個別株、例えば、アマゾンやマクドナルドなどを買って、業種はバラバラにして自分で安定させるのです。
You buy individual stocks such as Amazon or McDonald's and then choose a variety of stocks in different industries to lower your risk.

例えば、政府がIT企業のアマゾンやグーグル系に独占禁止法など
を理由に罰金を科したとしてその株が下がっても、スーパー系、
建築系、金融系、などはまた違った動きをするので、混ぜれば
一気に下がることはありません。

For example, let's say IT companies such as Amazon or
Google get penalized by the government under antitrust
law. Their stocks would plummet, however, the prices of
other stocks such as grocery stores or construction or
financial industries move differently, so if you have a
mixed bag of those, your investment balance would not
fall so significantly.

それを自分でバランスを取って、リスクを小さくします。
So, you make a balanced portfolio and minimize risk.

要するに、個別株を色々買って投資商品を作るというように、
大手の証券トレーダーの気分を味わいます。
To put it simply, you pretend that you are a stock trader
who belongs to a major investment company by
choosing individual stocks to make a product.

今日はリスクレベルのことについてですが、リスクの低い順は
こうです。
Today I am explaining risk level, and the order from least
risky to most risky is as follows.

（１）ミューチュアルファンド/ETF（証券会社で買える株の集
まり）
(1) Mutual Fund / ETF (investment product you can buy
from an investment company)

（２）手作りミューチュアルファンド （個別株を自分で選ぶ）
(2) Handmade mutual fund (you choose individual stocks)

（３）個別株 - 配当金のある歴史の長い会社。マクドナルドなど

(3) Individual stocks - stable companies with long histories that pay out dividends such as McDonald's

（４）個別株 - 配当金がないけれど、成長しているGAFA (Google, Amazon, Facebook, Apple) のような株 *Apple は配当しています。

(4) Individual stocks - rapidly growing companies such as those in GAFA (Google, Amazon, Facebook, Apple) *Apple does pay out dividends.

高校生にも分かるように説明しているのですが、株を買っているみなさんはどのように投資をしていますか？

I am explaining stock investment in a way even high schoolers can understand, but to those who are already buying stocks, how's your portfolio?

第4章 - 日本の若者は投資の勉強ができない
CH4 - It's Hard for Young Japanese to Learn Stock Investment

投資の勉強って、やっぱり実際に買ってみるのが一番です。
The best way to learn about investment is to invest.

だけど、日本の若者は、株を買う練習が簡単にできなくてかわいそうだと思います。
However, I feel sorry for young Japanese people because it's not that easy to buy stocks to learn about how it all works.

アメリカの株は一株から買えるけれど、日本の株は１００株まとめてじゃないと買えないからです。
American stocks are sold by individual units, however, Japanese stocks are sold by 100 units.

例えば、ユニクロの株を買うには、今現在67,150円だから、671万円払わないと買えません。（2019年12月18日付）
For example, in order to buy UNIQLO stock, one unit of stock is currently ¥67,150, so you would need to pay ¥6,715,000 yen (Approx., $67,150) initially.

この仕組みを作った人って、誰なんでしょう？
Who made this rule?

アメリカでは、例えば10ドルの株を一つ買うと、手数料が7ド
ルとかかかるから確かに意味がないけど、株の勉強にはなりま
す。
In America, let's say you buy a stock at $10, you must
pay a transaction fee of the $7, so it's not reasonable to
make a profit, but you can still learn from it.

やっぱり実際に買うと、時々株の値動き（相場の上がり下が
り）を見るようになるから、勉強になるんですね。
After all, if you buy it, you will check the stock price trend
constantly, so you will learn how stock prices move.

こういうことがあったから、デジタル系の株が落ちたとか、FRB議長（アメリカの連邦銀行のリーダー）がFOMC（その定例ミーティング）でこういう発言をしたから、何系の何の株が下がったとか、少しはニュースに耳を傾けるようになるんです。
This incident made IT-related stocks fall, or FRB chairman said this on FOMC, so this industry's stock fell or so on.

私の投資はほとんどがミューチュアルファンドですが、始めは個別株を買うのは怖かったので、100ドルくらいから買って勉強して増やしました。
Most of my investments are mutual funds. It was scary to buy individual stocks initially, so I started with $100 individual stock investments, and made them bigger.

アメリカから帰ってきて、楽天証券に口座を作ってみましたが、結局日本の株を買う気にはなりませんでした。
I opened an investment account with Rakuten Investment Company when I came back from America, however in the end, I did not feel like buying any Japanese stock.

日本でも米国株を買えます。いろんなルールがありますが、手数料は大体2000円くらいだと思います。
You can buy U.S. stock in Japan. There are several rules though the transaction fee is approximately ¥2,000 for each transaction.

クレジットカードが作れる人でないと証券会社の口座も開けませんが、高校生でも条件付きで投資ができるようです。それにしても、何百万円単位の投資は難しいですよね。
If you don't have credit card, it's difficult to open an investment account, but a high school student can open

an account under certain conditions. Even so, the
investment of a few ¥,1000,000 (about $10,000) would
be difficult.

手数料はともかく、一株から買える米国株から練習してみると
いいと思います。
Regardless of the transaction fee, I recommend you
learn how to buy stock by investing in individual U.S.
stocks.

第5章 - 証券口座を開いてみる
CH5 - Opening Investment Account

私の父は、アメリカ企業の日本支店で働いていて、上司もアメリカ人だったのに、日本支店だったので、４０１Ｋなどのサポートはありませんでした。
My dad used to work at an American company, however, it was the Japanese branch, so there was no retirement plan such as 401k.

それもあって株には懐疑的で、やはり「株はギャンブルみたいなもんだろう」という考えでした。
As such, he was so skeptical when it came to investing in stocks that he thought, "Buying stocks is almost like gambling".

しかし最近の投資ブームからか、リタイヤして暇だからか、突然株に興味を持ったようです。
However, now he is interested in buying stocks probably because of the recent investment boom in Japan, or he has plenty of time now that he is retired.

「花子、お前最近株の買い方ビデオやってるらしいな。
お父さんも、ちょっとやってみたいんだけど。何買ったらいいか、教えてくれない？」と、言ってきました。
"Hanako, I heard you are making videos about how to buy stocks. I want to try it, can you tell me how?"

私は証券口座がアメリカの口座なので、具体的にみなさんに教えるためには日本の楽天証券などから米国株を買ったほうがいいと思って口座は開けたものの、やっぱりアメリカに税金を払っている私はちょっと納税が面倒になるため楽天証券からは買いませんでした。
My investment account is in America, so I opened the account with Rakuten Investment in Japan, however, I haven't bought any stocks through Rakuten since tax payment would be complex for me.

これは都合がいいモニターがきた。
I thought my dad would be a great monitor.

「よっしゃ、ネギが鴨を背負ってやってきた！！」
"Yes, green onion came carrying a duck!!"

と言ったものの、なんか変だと思ったら逆だった。
I said that, but I realized it's the opposite.

「カモがネギ背負ってやってきた」だったね。。。
The correct saying is, "A duck came carrying green onion".
(It's a Japanese saying, meaning something convenient came with another convenient thing.)

しかし、料理できるカモとネギが一緒に来たということで、理論的にはどちらでもいいってことですよね？
But it's same meaning logically since the duck and green onion both came together.

私、日本語の先生をやっている割には、こういう間違いが多いんです。
I made such mistakes although I am a Japanese teacher.

話が逸れましたが、、、
Back to the topic,

とにかく、株初心者モニター（父）ゲット！ということで、
I got a stock investment monitor (my dad)! And on that note,

この貴重なモニターの気が変わる前に、、、と、怪しい証券会社スタッフのように、勧誘に入りました。
I tried to convince him to start investing before he changes his mind as if I were an investment salesperson.

父「いや、なんか株買うのも面白そうだと思ってさ！まずは20万円くらい無くなった、と思ってやってみたいんだけど～。」
My dad: "Well, I thought it might be interesting to buy stocks! I would like to start with about ¥200,000 initially since it's ok for me if I lose that amount.

花子「で、どんな株にご興味が？個別株？投資信託？」
Hanako: "So, what kind of stocks are you interested in? Individual stocks or mutual funds?"

父「やっぱり、個別株がいいよねー。上がったり、下がったり見るの面白いじゃん。」
Dad: "I decided I want to buy individual stocks. It's fun to see it go up and down."

花子「なるほど、なるほど。おっしゃる通り。」
Hanako: "I see, I see. I agree."

父「日本の株をさ〜」
Dad: "I want to buy Japanese stocks".

花子「いやいや、お客さん。日本の株は１００株単位じゃないと買えないから、20万円でも結構個別株を買うのは難しいんだよね〜。」
Hanako: "No, no, dear customer. You have to buy a bundle of 100 stocks if you want to buy Japanese stock, so it would be difficult to buy those even if you have ¥200,000 to invest.

例えばユニクロ株は一株６万円以上だけど、１００株単位で買わないといけないので、最初から６００万円だよ。
For example, one stock of Uniqlo is more than ¥60,000, and you have to buy a 100-stock bundle so the initial payment would be ¥6,000,000 (about $60,000).

米国株はどうですか？米国株は一株単位で買えるんですよ～。だから、10ドルの株を一つでも買える。日本の株だと、なかなか選ぶのが難しいし、市場としてはアメリカの株のほうがいいですよ。」
How about U.S. stocks? You can buy them individually. So, you can buy one stock for $10. If it were Japanese stock, it's hard to find good stock with a lower price, and after all, the American stock market is better than the Japanese one. "

父「確かに、アメリカはどんどん上がっているらしいからな～。じゃあ、アメリカの株で。」
Dad: "You are right. I heard U.S. stock prices have been going up. So, I will buy U.S. stocks."

花子「なるほど、なるほど。手数料は一回の取引ごとに、10ドルから20ドルだと思うんだけど、複数買ったほうがいいと思うんだよね。」
Hanako: "I see. The transaction fee could be $10 to $20 though, I think you might want to buy multiple stocks."

父「じゃあ、5万円くらいを四種類買うっていうのはどうかな～？」
Dad: "Then how about buying four kinds of stocks for ¥50,000 each?"

花子「いや〜、なかなかいいですよ〜。それでは、早速お手続きの方は私がネットでチャチャっと済ましちゃうんで、健康保険証とマイナンバー貸してもらえますか〜？」（気が変わらぬうちに、さっさと必要なものを徴収）
Hanako: "Well, that's pretty good. So I will do the application quickly online, can you give me your medical insurance card and your "Individual Number Card" that the government issued you. (Before he changed his mind, I quickly collected the required information).

母「大丈夫なの〜？なくなるかもしれないんだったら、好きなもの買ったほうがいいんじゃない？」
Mom: "Is it safe to invest? If there is a possibility you will lose it all, why not spend the money on something you like?"

花子：「（商売の邪魔だな〜。とにかくこのモニター（父）を安心させて。。。）大丈夫ですよ！個別株は、いつでも引き落としできるから、やめたくなったらいつでもやめればいいし。税金だって、儲けがあって引き落とした時だけ払えばいいんだから。そんな急激に株価が落ちることないから、損しないって〜！大体、リタイヤしてやることないんだから、ちょっと趣味が増えて時間つぶしになるじゃん。」
Hanako: "(She is intruding in my business. Anyways, I must persuade this customer…) It's all right! You will be able to cash out the individual stock anytime you like, so whenever you want to stop investing, you can! If you make a profit, you will be required to pay the taxes. U.S. stock price won't drop significantly, so you won't really lose anything. Pretty much, you don't have anything to do after the retirement, so you can spend time investing in stocks.

ということで、、、
So on that note,

いや、モニターゲット、という目的があるから、怪しい証券マンのようになりましたが、上記は全部本当のことなので、安心してください。
I may have sounded like a shady investment salesperson, however, everything I said is true, so please don't worry!

ということで、楽天証券にオンライン申し込みしました
So I applied for a Rakuten investment online for my dad.

申し込み途中で、「積み立てNISA（少額非課税制度）」や「IdeCo(個人型確定拠出年金)」勧誘はありますが、ここはとりあえず無視。後で入りたければ入ればいいです。
While you proceed with the application, they recommend you to start NISA (something like IRA) and IdeCo, but let's ignore that for now.

保険証の裏表をスマホで撮って、アップロード。
Take a picture of your medical insurance card front and back, and upload it on their website.

これで、ログイン名とパスワードが郵送で届きます。
Now they are going to send you your login information by mail.

私も楽天証券に申し込みしました。
I also completed the application with Rakuten.

ログインとパスワードが郵送で一緒に届く、ということが意味不明。。。
I don't understand why they send your password together with your login info in the mail…

アメリカでは絶対にありえないと思うんですが。。。
I don't think something like that would happen in America…

それ郵便受けから盗まれたらどうすんの？
What would you do if your mail gets stolen?

まあ、盗まれてもそのあとマイナンバー登録をしないといけないので大丈夫なんでしょうが。
Well even if it was stolen, the My Number registration should still be required, so it's all right.

あ、楽天証券申し込む人で、マイナンバー取っていない人は、市役所、町役場、区役所、で、登録しないと申し込みできませんよ〜。
Oh! For applicants who do not have a My Number, you will need to register at your municipal office, town hall, or ward office.

第6章 - FXは好きじゃないけど
CH6 - I don't Like Dealing with the FX Market, But

私はFXはあまり好きではないのでやっていません。
I don't really like FX trading so I never do it.

市場の動きは予想ができても、短期勝負なのでなかなか確実に
儲ける方法は難しいです。
It's difficult to make a stable profit from FX even if you
try to predict the market because it's such a short-term
investment.

ところで「日銀砲」って聞いたことがありますか？
By the way, have you heard of "Nichigin-Hou"?

FXは操作されることがあるけれど、「操作する奴らを潰したこ
の話はかっこいい！」と思いました。
FX could also be manipulated, but I always like to hear
about those manipulators getting crushed.

日銀砲とは、日本銀行(日銀)による直接または間接的な為替市場
介入です。
"Nichigin-Hou" is the direct and indirect FX market
intervention by the Bank of Japan.

2001年のアメリカ同時多発テロの頃、禿鷹ファンドと呼ばれる
アメリカの投資家が相場の操作のために円を買い占めたんです。
In the year 2001 in the United States, when the 9/11
terrorist attacks occurred, American investors, called the
"Hagetaka Fund" ("vulture" fund), bought a large amount
of yen in order to control the FX market.

すると市場に出回る円が少なくなり、円高になるので、そこで
手持ちの円を売って次はドルを買います。
The yen in the market had decreased in value
significantly, so the Japanese yen could only increase in
value from there, so those "Hagetaka Fund" sold the yen
and bought dollars.

こうやって市場の相場を釣り上げては売って、その差額で儲け
ていました。
They raised the price of currency in the market so that
they could sell it and then profit from the difference.

そこで日本が困ることは何か？
So what would be the problem for Japan?

円が高くなると、日本が海外に輸出している企業は売れなくな
ります。
When the value of yen gets higher, Japanese exports
would decline.

そこで2003年末ごろから介入したのが財務省の谷垣さんで、実
際に行動したのは当時の日銀総裁、福井俊彦さんです。
Around 2003, Mr. Tanigaki of Japan's Ministry of Finance
began the FX market intervention, and Mr. Toshihiko
Fukui, the President of the Bank of Japan, directly took
action.

その介入のかっこいいこと！
The intervention was so cool!

一日24時間、１分に１０億円を売って、円を売りまくり、円安にしたんです。
They started selling 1,000,000,000 yen (about $10 million) per minute and lowered the yen.

そしてドルを買いまくり、禿鷹ファンドの邪魔をしました。
Then, they started buying US dollars to interrupt the activity of the Hagetaka Fund.

手持ち３０兆円が尽きると財務省が保有している200兆円もの米国債を幾らか売って弾を込めたと考えられてます。
When they used $300 billion of the Bank of Japan, they sold part of $2 trillion of US Treasury stock and continued buying US dollars.

これを３５日間続けました。
They continued doing it for 35 days.

そして、アメリカのヘッジが2000社倒産したと言われます。
Then, people say about 2,000 American hedge companies went bankrupt.

これができるのは、日本の手持ちのお金が大きいからですね。日本の株はイマイチですが、財政的には安定した国ですよ。
It was possible because Japan has a lot of cash. Although Japan's stock prices were not doing well, Japan is a financially stable country.

年金もあまり心配いらないんじゃないんでしょうか？
I am optimistic about Japan's pension payout.

この日銀の行為は反則ギリギリですが、禿鷹ファンドを潰すために必要だったと思います。
Although what the Bank of Japan did was borderline illegal, it was necessary to fight back against the Hagetaka Fund.

この後から日本円を狙うのは無謀だという考えが世界に広まりました。
As a result, people all over the world believed it reckless to attack the Japanese yen thereafter.

日銀は世論的には馬鹿にされている風潮もありますが、私はこの話は格好いいので、鳥肌が立ちます。
Many Japanese people tend to think that the Bank of Japan lacks ability, however, I get goose bumps when I hear this cool story.

どうせFXをするなら、こんな操作をしてみたいもんですね。
If I deal with FX. I would like to do this kind of FX market intervention.

禿鷹ファンドをぶっ潰す日銀側がいいですけど。
I prefer to do the kind of intervention that the Bank of Japan used to attack the Hagetaka Fund though.

第7章 - 「高校生のうちに買っておいた方がいい株はありますか？」
CH7 - Any Stocks That High School Students Should Buy Now?

こんな質問を受けました。
I received a question like this.

「現在高校生なのですが、今のうちに持っておいたほうがいい株ありますか？？」
"I am a high school student. Is there any stock I should buy now?"

【わたしの答え】
[My reply]

オススメしたい株はいろいろありますが、基本米国株です。
There are many stocks I would like to recommend, but basically, I recommend you to buy U.S. Stocks.

日本株は調べたけど、買う気になりませんでした。
I did research about Japanese stocks, but I decided not to buy any.

これがいい、と言っても責任とれませんので、まずは世界一の投資家、ウォーレン・バフェットが何を買っているかみてください。
Even if I say, "Buy this stock", I can't take responsibility, so first, please take a look at the stocks the world's best investor, Warren Buffet, buys.

ウォーレンバフェットの保有株トップ10

2019年4月付で、1番はアップルの約5兆円です。
The highest stock he has is Apple, amounting to $48.9 billion as of 4/2019.

【As of 4/2019】

	Symbol	Holdings	Mkt. price	Value ▽	Stake
TOTAL				$203,113,700,532	
Apple Inc.	AAPL	249,589,329	$195.95	$48,907,029,018	5.4%
Bank of America Corp	BAC	896,167,600	$28.02	$25,110,616,152	9.4%
The Coca-Cola Co	KO	400,000,000	$51.07	$20,428,000,000	9.4%
American Express Company	AXP	151,610,700	$122.30	$18,541,988,610	18.2%
Wells Fargo & Co	WFC	409,803,773	$45.20	$18,523,130,540	9.1%
Kraft Heinz Co	KHC	325,634,818	$30.43	$9,909,067,512	26.7%
U.S. Bancorp	USB	129,308,831	$52.76	$6,822,333,924	8.1%
JPMorgan Chase & Co.	JPM	59,514,932	$109.48	$6,515,694,755	1.8%
Moody's Corporation	MCO	24,669,778	$190.01	$4,687,504,518	13.0%
Delta Air Lines, Inc.	DAL	70,910,456	$56.86	$4,031,968,528	10.8%

(Refer to: CNBC Warren Buffett Watch)

2018年12月には、アップル株がどーんと下落したので、バフェットはネットで叩かれましたが、2019年11月時点はこうです。
As of December 2018, Buffett was criticized online for having more than ¥5 trillion (about $50 billion) in Apple stock since the price tumbled, however the value as of November 2019 was as follows.

【As of 11/2019】

	Symbol	Holdings	Mkt. price	Value	Stake
TOTAL		3,503,097,197		$243,416,595,384	
Apple Inc.	AAPL	248,838,679	$279.86	$69,639,992,705	5.6%
Bank of America Corp	BAC	947,760,000	$34.70	$32,887,272,000	10.5%
Coca-Cola Co	KO	400,000,000	$54.42	$21,768,000,000	9.3%
Wells Fargo & Co	WFC	378,369,018	$54.22	$20,515,168,156	8.9%
American Express Company	AXP	151,610,700	$123.68	$18,751,211,376	18.5%
Kraft Heinz Co	KHC	325,634,818	$31.74	$10,335,649,123	26.7%
JPMorgan Chase & Co.	JPM	59,514,932	$137.34	$8,173,780,761	1.9%
U.S. Bancorp	USB	132,459,618	$60.66	$8,035,000,428	8.5%
Moody's Corporation	MCO	24,669,778	$236.10	$5,824,534,586	13.1%
Goldman Sachs Group Inc	GS	18,353,635	$228.04	$4,185,362,925	5.2%

どんなに叩かれてもほとんど売っていないから、５兆円から７兆円と、ほぼ２兆円増えました。
He did not sell most of the Apple stock despite of the criticize, so the value rose by about ¥2 trillion (about $20 billion) from ¥5 trillion (about $50 billion) to ¥7 trillion (about $70 billion).

実際一番安全なのは、ミューチュアル・ファンドやETF、いわゆる投資信託、株のまとまりですが、大きく当てたい場合は個別株を買います。
Really the safest ones are mutual funds or ETFs, bundles of stocks, but if you want to hit it big, investment in individual stocks would be recommended.

まずは日本のNikkei 株指標（株のまとまり）の過去の動きアメリカのS&P（株のまとまり）の傾向を見てみましょう。
First, let's look at stock price trends in Japan's Nikkei Stock Index (bundle of stocks) and America's S&P stock index (bundle of stocks).

<Nikkei Index - Japan> As of 12/2019

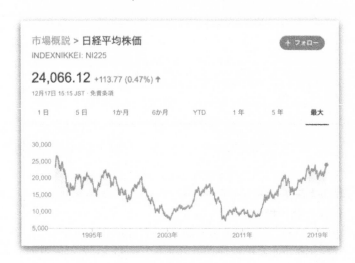

<S&P 500 - America> As off 12/2019

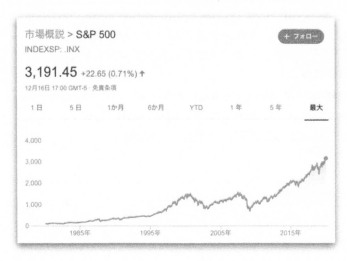

もしあなたが、日本のインデックス株を20年前に1,000万円分買っていたら、それは今も1,000万円です。
If you purchased $100,000 of Japanese Index stocks 20 years ago, you would still have $100,000 today (based on conversion rate of ¥100/ per US dollar).

もしあなたがアメリカの株のまとまり（インデックス株）1,000万円分を20年前に買っていたら、それは今は約4,000万円になっています。
If you purchased $100,000 of American Index stocks, it would now be $400,000.

アメリカは、世界のGDPでみても世界一です。
Even when you look at global GDP, America is number 1 in the world.

しかし、こんなに小さい島国、日本の経済は、世界３位です。
But, the small island nation of Japan ranks number 3.

2020年は東京オリンピックがありますが、選手の行進って長すぎると思いませんか？
The Tokyo Olympics will be held in 2020, though, the entry march of the opening ceremony is too long, isn't it?

世界に国は何個あるんだろう？
How many countries are there in the world?

196国ですよ！
196 countries!

日本も頑張っていますよね〜。
Japan is doing a very good job.

第8章 - アナリストの意見は聞くな
CH8 - Don't Follow Analysts' Opinions

私は、買おうか買わないほうがいいか、という時にはアナリストの意見は、まず聞きません。
I never listen to analysts' opinions when I decide whether or not to buy a certain stock.

アメリカの有名な証券アナリストの意見で今が「買い」か「売り」か、というものが買いてあると思いますが、それが当たった試しがありません。
You can often see famous analysts label certain stocks as "must buy" or "must sell", but in my opinion, their recommendations have not always been correct.

例えば、今1株が1800ドルくらいになっているアマゾン株ですが（2019年12月付）、私は250ドルの時に買いました。
For example, the stock price of Amazon is currently around $1800 (as of Dec 2019), but I bought it when it was still $250.

その時のアナリストの意見なんてひどいものでしたよ。
The analysts' views on the Amazon stock at the time were terrible.

250ドルのときは、アマゾンが海外ビジネスを広げていて、資産投資が多かったため、最終損益を出し株が下がりました。
When the price was $250, Amazon was trying to expand their business to overseas markets, and as a result, they spent a lot of capital investment, then posted a net loss

市場概説 > Amazon.com

+ フォロー

NASDAQ: AMZN

1,769.21 USD +8.27 (0.47%) ↑

営業終了: 12月17日 5:34 GMT-5・免責条項
時間前取引 1,770.00 +0.79 (0.045%)

| 1日 | 5日 | 1か月 | 6か月 | YTD | 1年 | 5年 | **最大** |

その時のアナリストの意見は、もうアマゾン株は上がっても
500ドルなど、ひどいものでした。
Analysts said amazon stock would never exceed $500.

今見てごらん、という感じですよ。
I want to say, "Look at the stock price now!".

なんなら、自分だけ儲けたいから本当のことを言わないのか？
とも思います。
Or maybe they intentionally said that so that they can
make more of a profit themselves?

また、2004年に私がアメリカにある日本の銀行で働き始めた時
に、トレーダーに「ネットフレックスは今が買い時じゃないです
かね？」と聞いたら、「あーあんなの、すぐ潰れる。宅配DVD
なんてだめだ。」と言っていました。
Also, when I started working at a Japanese bank in
America in 2004, I asked one of the bank traders

something along the lines of, "Isn't Netflix a must-buy right now?", however, he said, "Oh no, they will be bankrupt soon. A DVD delivery service simply cannot work".

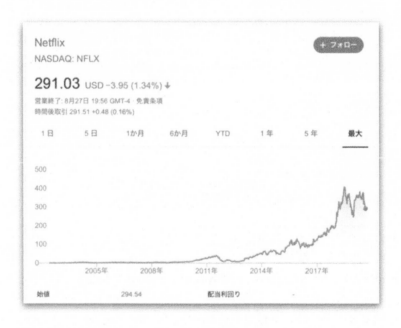

そのとき一株５ドルだったけれど、今は360ドルです。10,000 ドル（100万円）買っていたら、7,200万円ですよ。
At the time, Netflix stock price was only $5, but now it's $360. If I had bought $10,000 in Netflix stock, it would have grown to $720,000.

何が言いたいかというと、「株を買うのに人の意見は聞くな。決算書を読んで自分の頭で考えろ。」です。
What I want to say here is, "Do not listen to someone's opinion when you buy stocks. Read the financial statements yourself and try to decide whether or not to buy using your brain".

株で儲ける為に、一番大事な事は、
The most important thing in profiting from stock investment is,

「自分の頭で考える。」です。
"to think by yourself".

だって、もし米国有名証券アナリストの意見を聞いたところで、それを読んでいる時点で他の人も読んでいるわけで、その時株を買おうとしても高くなっています。
Even if you listen to famous U.S. investment analysts' opinions, everyone else knows too if they read the same article, and it will already be too late as prices will already be going up by then.

私が思うには、今まで結構儲かった株で彼らの意見が正しかったことはあまりないです。
In my opinion, when I make a lot of profit, it's when I don't listen to analysts.

一番儲ける秘訣は、ちょっと株のことを知っている人が「え？その株を今買う？もう終わっているよ。」とか、
「その株は絶対上がらないね。」と言っている時に買うことです。
The secret to making a profit is, it's the right time to buy when others who have a bit of knowledge in the stock market say, "Huh? You're buying that now? It's too late, you know.", or, "That stock will never rise."

だって、だからみんなその株を買わないから一株が安くて、あとで業績が良くなった時にガーンと株価が上昇するから。
It's because the majority of people don't buy the stock so then the stock price goes down, and when the financial result turns out to be good, the stock price will soar.

人と同じ動きをしていたら、がっつり儲けることはできません。
If you follow what other people do, you can't really make a large profit.

同時に、人と違う動きをしているから、ドーンと損をすることもあるんです。
At the same time, there is a possibility you will lose a lot if you don't follow other people.

損をしないように自分で考える為には、まず決算書を読めるようにならないといけません。
In order to think by yourself to avoid losing money, you need to be able to read financial statements.

これはレポートを作るわけではないので、簡単です。
It's easy since you are not making a report.

そして、証券アナリストにできなくて、あなたにできること。
And there is one thing you can do that investment analysts can't.

消費者として、その会社が好きかどうかを考える。
You consider if you like the company as a consumer.

例えば、アマゾンが伸びるな、と思った理由は、これです。
For example, the reason why I thought Amazon would expand on this.

ちょっと何年か忘れましたが、インターネットのスピードが遅くて画像のダウンロードに時間がかかった時代。
I forgot when, but I remember it was a time when it took a long time to upload pictures due to slow internet speeds.

2005年くらいかな〜。。。
Maybe it was around 2005…

アマゾンの株が今は1,800ドルですが、当時は10ドルでした。
The stock price of Amazon is currently $1,800, but at the time, it was only $10.

その頃、こぞって素敵なホームページを作る会社が多い中、アマゾンは素敵なホームページをできるにも関わらず、画像をあまり入れていないダサいホームページにしていました。
At the time there were many companies who created their own wonderful homepages. Amazon was able to make a great webpage, but there were not many pictures and it was kind of old-fashioned.

ホームページを開けるたびに、「アマゾンって伸びる！」と思いました。
Whenever I accessed the homepage, I thought, "Amazon will surely grow!".

だって、早くページが開いて、イライラしないんですから。
It's because the page always loaded quickly so I was not irritated.

あとは個人的な注目株はアルファベット（グーグルの会社）。
Another stock I am interested in is "Alphabet", which is
the parent company of Google.

ここには1000万円買ってもいいかな、と最近思っています。
Recently I am thinking about buying ¥10,000,000 of
stock.

どうしてかというと、アルファベットはユーチューブも持ってい
ますが、来年から５Gになってライブストリームが止まらなくな
るからです。
The reason is because Alphabet owns YouTube, and
streaming will definitely improve with the emergence of
5G.

私は2年前からユーチューブでライブストリームをしているので
すが、これが全く止まらなくなったらかなり助かります。
I have done live streams on YouTube. I think it would help
my business if it does not stop at all.

そして、テレビは衰退し、ユーチューブなどの動画に移動してお
り、これはどんどん加速しています。
Moreover, people are watching less and less television
and are watching more and more videos online like sites
like YouTube.

現に、最近ではテレビ局の闇が暴露されていますよね。
Pretty recently, TV stations' inappropriate acts are being
discovered.

それもこれも、ユーチューブで一般人が声を上げることができるようになったからです。
It's because ordinary people can now raise their voice through YouTube.

話は戻りますが、こうやって自分の生活の中で、どの会社が好きか、を考えればいいんです。
Back to the topic, you can choose which company you like personally.

もちろん上で述べたことは、アナリストなどの意見は全く入れていません。
Of course, I did not listen to any analyst's opinion for the above topic.

自分の客としての考えです。まずはどの会社が便利か、役になっているか、を考えたら、寝る時間もなくヘトヘトになっている米国有名証券アナリストに勝つのは簡単です。
It's my idea as a customer. First, think about if the company's products or services are convenient, if it is helping you, and if it's easy to win over the famous U.S. investment analysts.

彼らはゆっくりする時間がないんですから。
They don't have time to relax.

第9章 - 今更聞けない！「上場」とは？
CH9 - It's Odd to Ask, "What Is Jou-Jou?"

高校生でも分かる米国株、というタイトルなので、今日は、「上場とは？」というお話をしたいと思います。
Since the title of this book is, "U.S. Stocks Even High School Students Can Understand", I would like to talk about "What is jou-jou?".

上場会社は、英語でいうとPublic CompanyとかListed Companyと言います。
"Jou-jou company" means "public company" or "listed company" in English.

「パブリックカンパニー」なので、公共の会社だよ、という感じです。
As the name implies, it is a company which is public.

一般の人たちが、買った分の株のオーナーになれる、ということです。
It means that whoever buys stocks of that company becomes the owner of that percentage of stocks owned.

ということは、、、会社はオーナーに対して、もちろん隠し事はできません。
That means the company cannot hide anything to its "owners".

ということで、、、四半期ごとに決算書を作って、ちゃんと報告しなければいけません。
That way, the company must report its financial results every quarter.

上場していない個人の会社だったら、決算書に間違いがあって
も、大丈夫です。
If the company was not a public company, it's all right
even if there are mistakes in the financial statements.

しかし、上場した会社が決算書を故意に多めの儲けを載せたり
したら、犯罪になるわけです。
However, if the public company added fake profit to the
financial statements on purpose, it would be considered a
crime.

それが「粉飾決算」と言います。
That is called "window-dressing".

また、もちろん会社のお金を個人的なことに使ったら、犯罪で
す。
Also, if you use the company's money for personal use, it
would be crime as well.

日産のゴーンさんを見れば分かりますよね？
You know what happened to Carlos Ghosn of Nissan?

株が下がる原因となる情報を隠して、その前に自分の株を売っ
て損をしないようにすることを、「インサイダー取引」と言いま
す。
If a company purposefully hides information that could
lower the company's stock value, and if it sells the stock
before the stock price goes down, it's called "insider
trading".

私が銀行でアナリストをしていた時は、自分が分析している会社と全く関係のない株を買っても、全部銀行に報告していました。
When I was a credit analyst at a bank, I was responsible for reporting my own stocks to the bank even if it has not relation to the accounts I was in charge of.

証券会社から銀行へ直接レポートが送られるか、頼んだらすぐレポートする、ような形になっていた銀行もありました。
Some investment companies sent my portfolio directly to the bank I worked at, or others had agreements so that whenever the bank requests my investment portfolio, they would send it.

こういうことも「インサイダー取引」をしないようにするためです。
These are some countermeasures to "insider trading".

上場した会社の決算期の一年分の決算書とそれに付随する補足内容は、アメリカでは10Kと言います。
The annual financial statements and supplement memos of public companies are called "10K" in America.

四半期は、10Qです。
Those of quarterly report are called "10Q".

日本では、「有価証券報告書」です。
In Japan, it's called "yuka shoken hokokusho".

銀行が会社にお金を貸す場合にも、決算書を提出してもらいますが、上場した会社はきちんとした決算書がありますが、上場していない会社だと結構適当だったりします。
When a bank lends money, those financial statements are required. Public companies have appropriate financial statements, however, the financial statements of non-public companies are often not so great.

決算書の種類は、３種類あります。
There are three types of financial statements.

（１）Audited - 監査法人がある程度内容が正しいことを保証した決算書。しかし、報告した会社の責任者に最終的に責任あり。
(1) Audited - Accounting firms assure that the financial statement is accurate according to U.S. auditing standards. However, the final responsible party is the company itself.

（２）Reviewed - 会計士がチェックしたけれど、できる範囲までしか正しいと言えない決算書。
(2) Reviewed - Accountants checked the financial report, however, they give limited assurance.

（３）Compilation - 会社内部で適当に作っても、誰も文句言えない。嘘かもしれない決算書。
(3) Compilation - Nobody can complain about the financial report even if it is created sloppily within the company. It might not be accurate.

なので、上場した会社は、『(1) Audited(監査された）』決算書しか認められません。
So, public companies can only prepare audited reports.

逆にいうと、Compilation は、嘘かもしれないのに、銀行がそれを信用してお金を貸さないといけません。
In other words, compilation reports could be a lie, however, banks have to trust them if they are going to lend money.

信用できない場合、保証を入れてもらわないといけない場合もあります。
If it's not trustworthy, there are cases where the company must also submit a letter of guarantee.

そういうことをきちんとしないで簡単にお金を貸すと、アメリカ当局の検査で指摘され、罰金になるリスクがあります。
If the bank lends money without considering those things, financial authorities might call them out for it and worst scenario, the bank has to pay a penalty.

ということで、上場した会社の決算書は、信用できるものなのです。
So, the financial reports of public companies are trustworthy.

クレジットアナリストにとっては、とてもありがたいもの。
Credit analysts are very grateful for this.

それをしっかり確認しない手はない、ということです。
You should also check these things in depth.

第10章 - これだけは必要な英語の会計用語
CH10 - Accounting Terms You Need to Know

普通に「売掛金」とか「買掛金」という言葉を使っていましたが、もし高校生だったらわからないかな？と思いました。
I use a lot of financial terms such as "Account Receivable" or "Account Payable" without explaining them, but I thought it may be difficult to understand for high school students.

例えば、友達に任天堂スイッチを一万円で売ることになったとします。
For example, let's say you agreed with your friend to sell them your Nintendo Switch for 10,000 yen.

まだお金をもらっていません。
You have still yet to receive 10,000 yen from your friend.

それを会計用語ではなんと言うでしょうか？
What would be the appropriate accounting term?

あなたにとって一万円は売掛金です。
10,000 yen would be Account Receivable for you.

友達にとって一万円は買掛金です。
10,000 yen would be account payable for your friend.

ということで、今日は、「絶対覚えないといけない会計用語」を説明したいと思います。
So, I would like to explain the "financial terms you must remember".

まあ、株を買うなら覚えないと、ということです。
Well, if you purchase stock, you have to memorize those anyway.

じゃあ、並べていきます。
Now, I will tell you those.

（１）連結貸借対照表
　　　Consolidated Balance Sheet

（２）連結損益計算書
　　　Consolidated Statement of Income

（３）キャッシュフロー
　　　Cashflow

（1） 連結貸借対照表

Consolidated Balance Sheet

Alphabet Inc.
CONSOLIDATED BALANCE SHEETS
(In millions, except share amounts which are reflected in thousands, and par value per share amounts)

	As of December 31, 2017	As of December 31, 2018
Assets		
Current assets:		
Cash and cash equivalents	$ 10,715	$ 16,701
Marketable securities	91,156	92,439
Total cash, cash equivalents, and marketable securities	101,871	109,140
Accounts receivable, net of allowance of $674 and $729	18,336	20,838
Income taxes receivable, net	369	355
Inventory	749	1,107
Other current assets	2,983	4,236
Total current assets	124,308	135,676
Non-marketable investments	7,813	13,859
Deferred income taxes	680	737
Property and equipment, net	42,383	59,719
Intangible assets, net	2,692	2,220
Goodwill	16,747	17,888
Other non-current assets	2,672	2,693
Total assets	$ 197,295	$ 232,792
Liabilities and Stockholders' Equity		
Current liabilities:		
Accounts payable	$ 3,137	$ 4,378
Accrued compensation and benefits	4,581	6,839
Accrued expenses and other current liabilities	10,177	16,958
Accrued revenue share	3,975	4,592
Deferred revenue	1,432	1,784
Income taxes payable, net	881	69
Total current liabilities	24,183	34,620
Long-term debt	3,969	4,012
Deferred revenue, non-current	340	396
Income taxes payable, non-current	12,812	11,327
Deferred income taxes	430	1,264
Other long-term liabilities	3,059	3,545
Total liabilities	44,793	55,164
Commitments and Contingencies (Note 9)		
Stockholders' equity:		
Convertible preferred stock, $0.001 par value per share, 100,000 shares authorized; no shares issued and outstanding	0	0
Class A and Class B common stock, and Class C capital stock and additional paid-in capital, $0.001 par value per share: 15,000,000 shares authorized (Class A 9,000,000, Class B 3,000,000, Class C 3,000,000); 694,783 (Class A 298,470, Class B 46,972, Class C 349,341) and 695,556 (Class A 299,242, Class B 46,636, Class C 349,678) shares issued and outstanding	40,247	45,049
Accumulated other comprehensive loss	(992)	(2,306)
Retained earnings	113,247	134,885
Total stockholders' equity	152,502	177,628
Total liabilities and stockholders' equity	$ 197,295	$ 232,792

< 資産 Asset>

１） 流動資産 Current Asset

1年以内にお金にできるもの
The assets that can be converted into cash within a year.

a) 現金 Cash

b) 売掛金 Account Receivable

売ったものに関して、あとでお金をもらうもの
What you have sold but are not yet
reimbursed for

    c) 在庫 Inventory

2) 固定資産 Non-Current Asset

    a) Property＆Equipment 土地建物設備

< 負債 Liability>

１）流動負債 Current Liability

1年以内に払わないといけないもの
Liabilities the company has to pay within a year

    a) 買掛金 Account Payable
      買ったものについて、後日払うべきもの
      What you have purchased and still need to
      pay for.

    b) 短期借入金 Short-Term Loan
      1年以内に返すローン
      Loan due within a year

  2）固定負債 Non-Current Liability

      a) Long-Term Loan長期借入金（１年以上
        に返すローン）

< 資本 Stockholder's Equity>

1）普通株式 Common Stocks

　　　権利の制限がない会社の一部の所有するもの
　　　Unrestricted ownership of a part of the
　　　company

2）利益剰余金 Retained Earning

　　　今までの損益の積み重ねから、配当金を引いたもの
　　　The amount of accumulated net income left over
　　　for the business after it has paid out dividends to
　　　its shareholders

（2）Consolidated Statement of Income
　　　損益計算書

Alphabet Inc.
CONSOLIDATED STATEMENTS OF INCOME
(in millions, except per share amounts; unaudited)

	Three Months Ended March 31,	
	2018	2019
Revenues 売上	$ 31,146	$ 36,339
Costs and expenses: 経費		
Cost of revenues 売上原価	13,467	16,012
Research and development 研究開発費	5,039	6,029
Sales and marketing 宣伝費	3,604	3,905
General and administrative 一般管理費	1,403	2,088
European Commission fine ヨーロッパコミッション罰金	0	1,697
Total costs and expenses	23,513	29,731
Income from operations	7,633	6,608
Other income (expense), net その他収入	2,910	1,538
Income before income taxes	10,543	8,146
Provision for income taxes 税金予想	1,142	1,489
Net income	$ 9,401	$ 6,657

1）売上 Sales

2）売上原価 Cost of Goods Sold (COGS)

　　　売っているものだけにかかった費用
　　　Cost to manufacture the goods

3）販管費及び一般管理費
　　Selling General and Administrative (SG&A) Expense
　　　　売上原価以外にかかったもの、例えば、宣伝費や電話代
　　　　など
　　　　Costs other than COGS, such as advertisement or
　　　　telecommunication expenses

4）営業利益 Operating Income

　　　営業からだけの利益。投資の利益や税金などは入らない。
　　　Profit only from operation. This excludes profit from
　　　investments or tax

5）当期利益/当期損益 Net Income/Net Loss

最終的なこの時期の利益
Final profit during this term

大まかに考えると、この辺が分かっていればいいかな、と思います。
Basically, it would be really good if you know these terms.

他にも細々ありますが。
There are more detailed accounting terms though.

米国株チャンネルは英語はついていませんが、興味のある方は下のリンクからどうぞ。
There is no English translation on my U.S. stocks YouTube channel, but if you are interested in it, please follow the link below.

https://www.youtube.com/c/高校生でも分かる米国株

第11章 - サイゼリヤ株は買わなかった
CH11 - I Did Not Buy Saizeriya Stock

日本に帰ってきて、びっくりしたことはこれです。
What surprised me when I came back to Japan was this.

「サイゼリヤのミラノ風ドリアが美味しいのに、なんで２８０円！？」
"Why is this Milano-style doria at Saizeriya (restaurant) so tasty yet only ¥280!? (about $2.80)."

ロサンゼルスは、本当に外食が高いです。
It's so expensive to eat out in Los Angeles.

人気のあるレストランにブランチをするために行列に並んで、３０００円くらい払って雰囲気はいいけど高いです。
If you go to popular restaurants in LA, the atmosphere is good but we pay about $30.

だからサイゼリヤの安さにはびっくりしました。
So I was surprised with the inexpensive price at Saizeriya.

この値段で、決算書はどうなっているんだろう？と調べました。
I wondered how they make a profit with such low prices, so I checked their financial statement.

その時点では、売り上げ、収益もいいし、バランスシートもしっかりしている！
At the time, the sales and profit were good and their balance sheet was stable!

自己資本もとても高い！
Their equity ratio was also very high!

いいじゃないの！
It looks great!

と思って株価の動きを見て、びっくり。
Then, I was surprised by the trend in stock price.

これくらいの決算書だったら、過去にもっと上がってもいいはずの時期にも大して上がってない。
With such a wonderful financial statement, the stock price should have been much higher, but it wasn't.

国によって、こんなに株価の上がり具合って違うんだ。。。
Now I know the stock price doesn't rise depending on the country.

と思って、がっかりして買うのはやめました。
So I was disappointed didn't end up buying the stock.

会社が頑張っても、国の力によって株価の上がりって違うのね〜、と思いながら、いつになったらサイゼリヤのミラノ風ドリアに飽きるんだろう？と思う花子でした。
I was thinking maybe the stock price doesn't soar depending on the country even though the company made a great effort, and was also wondering when I will get bored of this Milano-style doria at Saizeriya.

第12章 - 証券会社が潰れた場合
CH12 - When Investment Companies Go Bankrupt

一応「高校生でも分かる」ということで書いているので、基本中の基本、税金についてです。
Since this book should be easily understandable to high school students, I will talk about the basic of basic: taxes.

高校生だから、意外と税金についてわからないんですよね。
It's somewhat difficult for high school students to understand.

100万円が1000万円になったとして、儲けは900万円じゃないですか。
If you invest one million yen, and it becomes 10 million yen, then the profit would be 9 million yen.

税金は儲け分の900万円にかかります。
The 9 million yen would be taxable.

税金が３０％だとしても、その株を引き落とししなければ、税金は払わなくていいんですよ。
Even if the tax rate is 30%, you don't need to pay the tax unless you cash out the profit.

900万円分引き落としたら、その30％（税率は人による）だとしたら、270万円。
If you cash out the 9 million yen, and if your tax rate is 30% (the tax rate will vary depending on your situation), the tax you pay is 2.7 million yen.

私の場合は、長期投資が主なものなので、税金は面倒ではありません。
My investments are mostly long-term investments, so tax is not that complicated for me.

逆に言えば、損していて引き落としたら、もちろん税金は払わなくてよし。
In other word, if you cash out the part of your investment that is not considered your profit, you don't need to pay tax on it.

それでは次に、証券会社が潰れた場合について説明します。
Now, I will explain the case in which the investment bank is bankrupt.

株を買ったことがない初心者の場合、特に長期的な投資の場合、何が心配か想像してみました。
I imagined what beginner investors might worry about, especially when it comes to long-term investment.

証券会社から株を買うことは説明しましたが、証券会社と言って思い出すのは、リーマンショックかもしれません。
I explained that we purchase stock through investment banks. When you hear "investment company", the name Lehman Shock might come to mind.

リーマンブラザーズは証券会社ですが、「もしリーマンブラザーズから株を買っていて潰れたら、その株は全部なくなってしまうんじゃないだろうか」と思ってしまうかも？
Lehman Brothers was an investment company, but you might wonder if you would lose all your investment if you purchase stocks through Lehman Brothers.

そんなことはありません。
It never happens.

買った株は証券会社の資産にはなっておらず、別管理になっています。
The stock you purchased is not posted as asset on the company's balance sheet.

会社が潰れたとしても、多少その日に売買ができなくなるという不具合があったとしても、買った株は他のところで管理されるだけです。
Even if the company goes bankrupt or there is some issue in trading that day, the purchased stock is just controlled in other areas.

とにかく、証券会社が潰れても、あなたの株は安全です。
Anyhow, even if the investment company goes bankrupt, your stock is safe.

第13章 - リスクの取り方
CH13 - How to Take Risks

実際株を買う時に大事なことは、リスクの分散です。あるいは、「どの程度のリスクを取っているか、自分でちゃんと理解していること」です。
Another important thing in buying stocks is to minimize risk, or, to know exactly how much risk you are taking.

「リスクと儲けとの関係は？」と聞かれたら、どう答えますか？
How would you answer if someone asked you, "How does risk relate to profit?"

リスクを取れば取るほど、大きく当たる可能性がある。
The more risk you take, the higher chance of hitting it big.

どうしてかというと、「大きく当たっている人というのは、人と違うことをしているから」です。
The reason why is that, "people who hit it big did something other people did not do."

じゃあなぜそれをみんなしないのか？
Then, why doesn't everybody do it?

「大きく外れる場合もあるから」です。
It's because "there are also cases where you can lose a lot".

ということは、「株で1日に数百万円　儲けました。」という人と同じくらい、「株で1日に数百万円　損しました。」という人がいるわけです。
That means, there are people who "made a few million yen profit in a day by investing stocks", but at the same time, there are also many people who "lost a few million yen in a day by investing stocks".

損した人の一部は、「株に手を出した馬鹿な自分。二度と投資なんてしない！」と考えてしまいます
Those who suffered such losses may think, "I am so stupid to start investing. I will never invest again!".

1日で数百万円損した人よりも、得した人の方が前面に出るので、「株を買ったら儲かる」と煽られる人もいます。
People who made a few million yen profit in a day shine more than people who lost a few million yen in a day, so some people believe the words of investment salespeople who say, "If you invest, I am sure you would make a profit."

ここで、損した人にも違いがあります。なんだと思いますか？
Now, there are differences among people who lose money. What do you think they are?

「損するかもしれないリスクは、十分織り込んでたので大丈夫」な人と、「損するなんていうパターンを考えていなかったので、生活できない状況に陥る。」です。
The two types are, "people who accept the loss since they understood the risk" and "people who never imagined that they could lose their money".

後者は「情報弱者」ということになります。
The latter group would be called "information poor".

じゃあなんで私が投資をすすめるのかというと、銀行にお金を
預けていても、利子がつかない。
So the reason why I recommend people to invest is that
even if you save money at a bank, you won't get interest.

しかも「毎年物価は上がる」ということは、現在のお金の価値
は、貯金していたらどんどん下がっていくということ。
On top of that, "consumer price is rising every year", so it
means that if you save money at bank, the value is
actually going down.

そして、銀行に貯金をしていると、あなたのお金をかき集めて
投資したり貸したりして　儲けるのはその銀行です。
And if you save your money in a bank, the bank collects
all their money from customers like you, and invests or
lends your money to make profit for themselves.

ということで、やはりお金を預けているだけで、利子ももらえ
ない自分は、銀行に利用されている情報弱者ということになり
ます。
That's why if you save money in a bank and don't get any
interest, you will be called "information poor".

リスクを最小限にして、とにかく安全をモットーに株を買うこ
とはできます。
There is a way to minimize the risk and invest in stocks
while having safety as a priority.

アメリカで働くと会社でサポートしてもらえる401Kというリタイアメントのサポートをしてもらえるのですが、（例えば、給料の５％をリタイアメントの投資に入れると、会社が同じ５％の金額を補填してくれる）その場合の投資はリスクの低い安全なものにします。

If you work in America, in most cases the company will provide you with a retirement plan called a 401K. (For example, if you invest 5% of your salary in retirement, and the company also contributes an additional 5% to match what you put in.

だからアメリカでは株はリスクが高いものではなく、将来のためにやっていて当たり前のものです。

So investment is not such a risky thing in America. It's common sense to do so for your future.

でも、夢を見たい人は、「リスクを認識して大儲けできそうな株の選び方」もできますよ。

However, if you want to hit it big, there is an option where you can aim to make lot of profit.

私が米国株を薦めている理由は、アメリカが経済大国第一位だから、必然的にリスクが一番低くて儲かる市場だからです。

The reason why I recommend that you invest in U.S. stocks is because America is economically the biggest country, so it's the least risky market.

どんなに決算結果が良い会社の株を買っても、その国の経済力がないと株価が伸びないんですよね。

Even if you purchase stocks of a company whose financial result was good, if the country was weak in terms of economy, the stock price would not go up very much.

今の所GDPによる経済大国ランキングは、以下の通り。
So far, the economical ranking by GDP is as follows.

＜2018年＞

順位	国名	単位：百万US$
1	米国	20,580,250
2	中国	13,368,073
3	日本	4,971,767
4	ドイツ	3,951,340
5	イギリス	2,828,833
6	フランス	2,780,152
7	インド	2,718,732
8	イタリア	2,075,856
9	ブラジル	1,867,818
10	韓国	1,720,489
11	カナダ	1,712,479
12	ロシア	1,657,290
13	スペイン	1,427,533
14	オーストラリア	1,420,045
15	メキシコ	1,222,053
16	インドネシア	1,022,454
17	オランダ	914,519
18	サウジアラビア	786,522
19	トルコ	771,274
20	スイス	705,546

来年2020年は東京オリンピックですが、入場行進は永遠に終わらないって感じじゃないですか？
Next year, year 2020, the Tokyo Olympics will be held. The entry parade of the opening ceremony continues forever, doesn't it?

だって、世界の国の数は196ヶ国ですよ？
There are 196 countries in the world, you know.

その中で資源もない島国日本が経済3位なんて、すごくないですか？
Don't you think Japan is doing quite well for a small island nation with minimal resources?

いや～、やはり日本の技術と勤勉さの賜物でしょうね。
Well, I think it's thanks to sophisticated Japanese technology and a hard-working culture.

実際、外国に長く住むと、日本の良さをしみじみと感じます。
Actually, if you live outside Japan, you would realize how good Japan is.

日本はもう終わりだ、と言う人たちも多いけど、そんなこと言わないで～！
Some Japanese people say, "Japan is so behind now", but don't say that!

日本にいると、日本の良さに気がつかないだけなのよ。
If you live in Japan, you won't notice how good Japan is.

と言いつつ、株はちゃっかり米国株を薦める私です。
But at the same time, I am saying that I recommend buying U.S. stocks when it comes to investment.

いや、日本はこれから、これから！
No, Japanese stocks will be better soon!!

日本の少子化を食い止めるために、私は日本で働ける外国人を教育していますから！
I am training non-Japanese to work in Japan to help counter the decreasing population issue of the country.

問題は、少子化ですからね〜。
The problem is Japan's population is declining.

話が逸れました。すみません。
But that's another topic, I am sorry.

上位５ヶ国の過去30年ほどの株価指数の動きを見てみましょう。
Let's take a look at the top 5 countries according to their stock index.

１）アメリカ
1) America

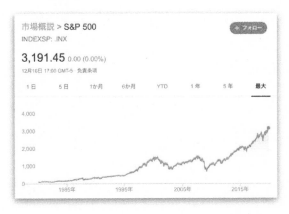

2008年のリーマンショックで落ちましたが、今はもう落ちた時からすると５倍くらいになっています。

The stock index declined in 2008 which was the time of "Lehman Shock", however, the stock prices now are five times higher.

2）中国

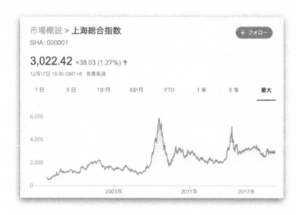

2007年に株価
が急に上がった
時に買った人
は、大変です
ね。
If you bought
this stock in
2007 when
the stock
price was that
high, I'm sorry.

3）日本
3) Japan

30年経って
も、まだ、過
去最高まで到
達していませ
ん。この
チャートを見
せたら日本政
府も、「老後
のために日本
の株に投資し
ろ」とは言え
ませんね。

After 30 years, the stock price has not yet returned to its once highest price. The Japanese government can't say "Invest on Japanese stocks" while showing this graph.

4）ドイツ

株価チャートは良さそうに見えますが、ドイツの経済は危ないと言われています。
The stock index looks good, however, people say that the German economy is on the edge.

そもそもがドイツ銀行の所有する証券資産の内容に問題があるようです。
It seems there is problem with the asset of securities Bank of Germany owns.

もしドイツの経済が落ちた場合、ドイツの大株主は中国ですから、大きく打撃を受けるとしたら中国じゃないですかね？
If the German economy declines, the majority of stock holders are in China, so it would get disadvantageous to them.

5）イギリス
5) U.K.

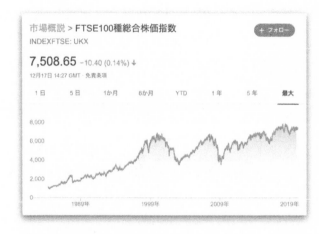

EU離脱する
とかしない
とか、メイ
首相頑張っ
たのに、何
も決められ
ませんでし
たね。

The former prime minister May did her best with Brexit, though nothing has been decided.

どうするんだろ？
I wonder what they are going to do.

（＊12/13/2019 付けでボリス・ジョンソンが首相に選ばれました。EU離脱も進みそうです。）
(*As of Dec 13, 2019, Boris Johnson was elected prime minister, and it seems that the Brexit will go on.)

世界の経済状況を私の目から見てどんな感じかということを簡単に言うと、
If you let me explain how the worldwide economic relationship is going,

アメリカは、中国が伸びないように監視していますし、
America is making sure China does not surpass them,

日本は、アメリカとうまくやっていて賢いけれど、株価の伸びはまだいまいち、
Japan is wise to be friend with America, but their stock prices aren't doing so well,

ドイツはドイツ銀行のバブル崩壊危機と言われており、
People say Bank of Germany's bubble is almost bursting,

「触らぬ神に祟りなし」と言う感じでしょうか。
It looks like, "sawaranu kami ni tatari nashi (If you don't deal with the god, you won't get cursed / Let sleeping dong lie)".

ドイツはアメリカが制裁を加えている中国と仲良くしているので、状況は悪化するばかり。
The German economy will get worse if it continues to be buddies with China while the U.S. is watching.

アメリカは、「中国と仲良しになる子たちとは、仲良くしない！」という主義ですからね。
America seems to think like, "If you become friends with China rather than us, we won't be so nice to you!".

アメリカは、ドイツとはどんどん距離を置いています。
America is distancing itself from Germany more and more.

アメリカが、「中国のHuawei（ファーウエイ）を使う子たちとは仲良くしない！」と言ったら、日本は慌てて中国通信企業のHuaweiを使わないことにしましたからね。
When America said, "If you use China's Huawei, we can't be friends!", Japan promptly decided not to use Huawei's services.

（米国は外国企業に対してファーウェイの製品やサービスを使う場合は罰金を課す計画をしている。）
(America plans to penalize any foreign companies using Huawei's products or services).

ドイツ潰れたら、EUは大変、ということで、、、
If German went bankrupt, it would be trouble for the E.U.…

イギリスもEU離脱するとかしないとか、、、EUにいても経済的にはろくなことはないだろうと思いますが。
The U.K. can't decide to exit from the E.U.. I assume if they stay with the E.U., it would not be good for their economy.

（* 12/13/2019 付けでボリス・ジョンソンが首相に選ばれました。EU離脱も進みそうです。）
(*As of Dec 13, 2019, Boris Johnson was elected prime minister, and it seems that the Brexit will go on.)

やっぱり一番の市場はアメリカだと思います。
After all, the American market is the best for investment.

ということで、私は米国株の紹介しかしておりません。
That's why I recommend you buy U.S. stocks only.

リスクを取ると言っても、市場は一番リスクが低いところにしたいので、まずは市場はアメリカです、というお話です。
My point is, even if you take risks, you should choose the least risky market which is America.

第14章 - 花子オススメ投資計画
CH14 - Hanako's Recommended Investment Plan

今日は、「花子のお勧め投資計画」についてお話ししたいと思います。
Today, I would like to talk about "Hanako's Recommended Investment Plan".

私は、「堅実、着実、確実」な投資をオススメしています。
What I recommend is, "Steady, Reliable, Certain" investment.

「株が儲かると煽られて、何百万円損して生活できない」と言う悲しい話を聞いたこともありますが、ちょっと知識を持てばそんなことにはなりません。
When I hear sad stories like, "Someone pushed me to invest because they said I can earn a lot of money, but I lost a few million yen. Now I don't even have enough money to live." If they knew a little more about investment, I don't think this would have happened.

一攫千金を狙うと、ろくなことはありません。
If you only dream about making a quick fortune, it probably won't end well.

2018年の年末あたりに、米国株が全体的に結構下がって、アップル株がどんどん落ちていったのを覚えていますか？
Do you remember when U.S. stocks plummeted at the end of 2018, and even Apple stock was on the decline?

5兆円越え(2019年12月現在7兆円）のアップル株を保有して
いる世界一の投資家、ウォーレンバフェットがネットで叩かれ
まくっていました。
Warren Buffett, the world's best investor, was criticized
online for having more than ¥5 trillion (about $50 billion /
about $70 billion as of Dec 2019) in Apple stock.

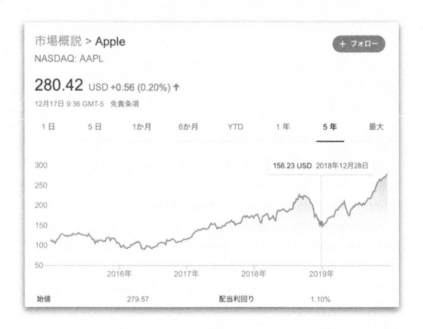

あの時、私は、「チャンス」と思って、アップル株を100万円分
買いました。
At that time, I thought, "Now's my chance!", and I bought
¥1 million (about $10,000) in Apple stock.

最高値が225ドルだったのが、156ドルまで落ちたので、
「よっしゃ！」と思って買いました。
The peak price was $225 and it dropped to $156, so I
thought, "Got ya!", and bought it.

でも世間はアップルを持っている人は馬鹿だと言う扱いですよ。
However, the general opinion was that people who still hold onto Apple stock are stupid.

でも2019年12月現在、280ドル。
But now it's $280 as of December 2019.

株価が下がる前の最高値を55ドルもアップしています。私が買った時よりも124ドル上がりました。
It's more than $55 higher than the highest price before the stock dropped. Compared to the price when I got, it increased by $124.

1年で79%のリターンです。
That's a 79% return in a year.

だけど、結構リスク取ってますよね？
However, I took a lot of risk, right?

世間ではアップルはもうダメだ、的でしたから。
It's because people thought Apple stock was no good then.

だけど、100万円の79%って79万円だけです。
However, 79% of ¥1 million is only ¥790,000 ($7,900).

1ヶ月に6万5800円儲かってるけど、これに税金３０％とか払わないといけないし。
That would be about ¥65,800 a month, but we have to pay like 30% in taxes.

これが1000万円だったら、790万円だったと言うのに！
If I had bought ¥10 million (about $100,000) of stock, I could have gotten ¥4.1 million yen (about $79,000)!

だから、正直言うと、最低でも1000万円以上はかけないと、9時ー5時で働かないでいいくらいにはならないんですよね。
So, to be honest, we should have at least bought ¥10 million (about $100,000) to free ourselves from having to work 9-5.

私は基本、アメリカの株で、長期投資をお勧めしています。
Basically, I recommend U.S. stocks as a long-term investment.

短期トレードはしていません。
I don't deal with short-term investment.

どうしてかと言うと、長期投資の方がコントロールしやすいからです。
The reason why is because it's easier to control long-term investment.

どうしてアメリカかと言うと、他のチャプターでもお話ししていますが、世界一の経済力なので、結局一番リスクが低いけれど、ハイリスク、ハイリターンの株も選べます。
The reason why it should be U.S. stock is because America is the world's biggest economic superpower, so it's lower-risk overall, yet, we can still choose high-risk high -return stocks if we want.

本物の金持ち、例えばウォーレンバフェットなども、長期投資で大金持ちです。
The real wealthy people such as Warren Buffett invest long-term.

私は、こう考えています。
I think like this.

高校生、大学生の場合、株で儲けようとしないで、数十ドルでもいいから買ってみて、株の動きを勉強したほうがいい。
If you are a high school student, or a college student, do not try to make a profit, rather, buy $10-$20 stocks and learn how they move.

働き始めた１０代、20代の人は、毎月貯金をすると思って株に投資したほうがいい。
If you are in your teens or 20's and just started working, invest in stocks as if you're saving money every month.

例えば、毎月3万円から5万円とか、株が多少上がったり下がったりしても、気にしないで毎月投資する。これは、アメリカの基本の考え方です。
For example, put in about ¥30,000 to ¥50,000 each month, ignore whether the stock goes up and down, and just keep investing. This is the fundamental American investment mindset.

そしてそれが、500万円、1000万円となったら、半分はリスクが高めな株などであげていく。
When total balance reaches ¥5 million (about $50,000) or ¥10 million (about $100,000), I recommend you invest in higher-risk stocks with half of your balance.

毎月4万円貯金したら、1年で48万円、10年で480万円です。
If you save ¥40,000 (about $400 per month), it would
become ¥480,000 (about $4,800) in 10 years.

私のリターンは平たくすると毎年２０％のリターンです。
My annual return averages to 20% every year.

ウォーレンバフェットもその年によって色々年率は変わります
が、平たくすると大体２０％のリターンで上がっています。
Warren Buffet's annual return changes every year,
though, his average is also about 20%.

２０％が無理だとしても５％だったら多少の知識で上げられま
す。
Even if an annual return of 20% is difficult, 5% should be
easy with some investment knowledge.

毎年５％で株が上がったとしたら、
If your stock rose by 5% every year,

【毎月4万円投資、５％リターンの場合】
Invest ¥40,000 every month with 5% annual return

Year	年の初め Beg of Year	リターン Annual Return	年の終わり End fo Year
1	480,000	5%	491,154
2	491,154	5%	1,007,437
3	1,007,437	5%	1,550,133
4	1,550,133	5%	2,120,595
5	2,120,595	5%	2,720,243
6	2,720,243	5%	3,350,570
7	3,350,570	5%	4,013,146
8	4,013,146	5%	4,709,620
9	4,709,620	5%	5,441,728
10	5,441,728	5%	6,211,291

毎月4万円10年貯金して、今は利子がないので480万円になり
ます。もし、毎月4万円を投資したら５％の利率で621万円にな
ります。
If you save ¥40,000 per month, it would become
¥480,000 in 10 years since there is no interest. If you
invest ¥40,000 a month with 5% annual return, it would
become ¥621,000.

その上、配当金も入りますよね。
In addition, you might receive dividends.

毎月4万円だったら、家のローンがあっても払えそうじゃないで
すか？
If it's only ¥40,000 each month, it looks doable even with
a housing loan.

ちゃんと勉強すれば、２０％にできます。
If you learn how to invest, you could make your annual
return 20%.

安定の２０％です。
It's a stable 20%.

20%だと毎月4万円投資して、10年でいくらになるか？
If you invest ¥40,000 per month with a 20% annual
return, how much would that be in 10 years?

約1,500万円です。
About ¥15,000,000 (about $150,000).

普通に毎月4万円貯金していたら、480万円です。
If you save ¥40,000 a month, it would be only
¥48,000,000 (about $480,000).

まずは、株の上がり下がりはあまり気にせず、1000万円を目指
して投資することをお勧めします。
First, I recommend you invest without worrying about
stock prices going up or down until your balance
reaches ¥10,000,000 (about $100,000).

ハイリスク、ハイリターンの株を始めるのは、その後でいいと思
います。
Then you can start some high-risk, high-return investing.

それからが勝負にはなるんですが、、
But that's when the battle begins.

そこで基本の株の選び方。
Now, let's think about how to choose stocks.

「株で儲ける」と言うのは、「優良(ブルーチップ)株を選ぶ」と言うことではないんです。
"Making a profit" does not mean "choosing blue chip stock".

株で稼ぐには、世間でダメだと思われている株の本質を見抜き、ダメな時に買わなければいけません。
In order to earn money from investing, you should find out the nature of the stock that everyone thinks is junk, and buy that when people still think it's garbage.

この本は、「高校生でも分かる米国株」なので、わかりやすい例を紹介します。
This book is titled "U.S. Stocks Even High School Students Can Understand", so I will show you a simple example.

例えば、
So for example,

親が銀行の頭取で、金持ち、東大卒のイケメンエリート男子。
There is an elite whose parent is the CEO of a bank, and he himself is a good-looking Tokyo University graduate.

彼が株だとしたら儲かると思いますか？
Let's say he is a stock, do you think you can make a lot of profit if you invest in him?

これは儲からないんです。
You cannot.

ホームレスみたいなボロボロの服を着た、モテなさそうな中年の中卒の男性が、自分で事業を起こし、年商100億を超えるビジネスにしたら？
Then there is a man who is middle-aged, looks homeless, has a middle school education, and does not look popular with women. What if one day he starts his own business and brings it to an annual profit of more than ¥1 billion (about $100 million)?

彼が株だったら、株価は1000倍です！
If he were a stock, the stock price would be 1000 times higher!

株でどかーんと儲けると言うことは、こう言うことです。
This is how you make a huge profit from investment.

しかし、東大卒のイケメンエリート男子はローリスク、ローリターンの優良株だとして、リスクが低いので買うと言うことはいいんですよ。
However, it's reasonable to buy the blue chip stocks (elite Tokyo University graduate). Although it's low return, the risk is low as well.

配当金も出ると思います。
You get dividends too.

でも、儲けはそれほどでもなく、普通から億万長者にはなれませんね。
However, the profit is not so huge, so the average person can't become a millionaire with that.

でも、誰が貧乏そうなボロボロの男性の本質を見抜いて、
1000万円かける？
But who wants to invest ¥10,000,000 on a man who
looks poor and wears dirty clothes?

危ないでしょう？
Isn't it dangerous?

だから、1000万円投資するなら、500万円はエリートイケメン
男性にかけて、500万円は貧乏そうだけど、あなたが信じた男
性を選びましょうってことですね。
Therefore, if you invest ¥10,000,000, I recommend you
invest ¥5,000,000 in the elite guy and another
¥5,000,000 on the guy who looks poor yet you believe in.

株の話なので男性の方が株に興味のある方が多いので、女性の
例を出したかったんですが、ちょっと例えが難しくなります
ね。
I wanted to show you an example about women since
generally guys are the ones interested in investment,
however, I couldn't think of a good example.

リスクの配分は自分の身を守るためにも大切です。
It's important to allocate risk in order to protect yourself.

２０代までのあなたは、まずは1000万円貯めましょう〜！
If you are in your 20's, let's save ¥10,000,000!

３０代以降のあなたも、まだだったら今からでも遅くない！
If you are in your 30's or older, and haven't saved
¥10,000,000 yet, it's not too late to do it!

第15章 - リーマンショックってなに？
CH15 - What Is "Lehman Shock"?

「リーマンショックみたいなことがあったら怖くて、株を買うのが怖い。」とよく聞きます。
People often say, "I'm afraid to buy stocks because I fear something like 'Lehman Shock' would happen again."

でもよーく突っ込んで聞いてみてください。
But try asking them about "Leman Shock" in depth.

結構リーマンショックについて分かっていない人、多いんですよ〜！
Many people don't know about "Lehman Shock" actually.

私もそういうワードを並べて、賢いフリをしたい時があるので、分かる分かる!
I understand that we want to use difficult terms and pretend to be smart!

そういうときは、「高校生でも分かる米国株」なんだから、分かるように説明しなくちゃ！と思います。
Then I think, the title is "U.S. Stocks Even High School Students Can Understand", so I need to explain it so they can understand!

あ、もちろん、分かってリーマンショックのことを言っている人もたくさんいますよ！
Of course, there are also many people who know about Lehman Shock!

そもそも、リーマンブラザーズ(証券会社) が倒産したのは、「サブプライムローン」をたくさん買って、それを売って儲けようとしたら、売る前に価値が無くなって潰れたんですよね。
Basically, the reason why the Lehman Brothers (investment company) went bankrupt was because they had bought a lot of "subprime mortgage" and aimed to make a large profit, however, those mortgages completely lost their value before they were able to sell them.

「サブプライムローン」については後ほど説明します。
I will explain "subprime loans" later.

詳しく知りたい方は、ブラッドピットが出ていた映画「マネーショート」を見ると分かりやすいです。
If you want to know about it, I think if you watch Brad Pitt's "Money Shot", it will be easier to understand.

あらすじには、こう書かれています。
The plot is like this.

「2015年アメリカ映画。マイケルルイスが著した本を原作に映画化した作品。リーマンショックが起きる前に経済破綻の危機に気づいた男たちの実話を、クリスチャン・ベイルやブラッド・ピットなど豪華キャストで描く。サブプライムローンの危険性を察知した金融トレーダーらが、ウォール街を出し抜こうとする様子を描く。この映画はアカデミー賞にもノミネートされました。」

"It's a 2015 American film based on the book written by Michael Luis. It is based on the true story of two men who noticed the economy bubble known as "Lehman Shock" before it burst. The main cast consists of famous actors such as Christian Bale and Brad Pitt. Financial traders who noticed the risks of "subprime loans" try to forestall others in the movie. This movie was nominated for an Academy Award. "

これを読んで、「異議あーり！」と思いました。
When I read this, I thought, "Objection!".

経済破綻の危機なら、たくさーんの人が気づいていましたよ。
There are many people who noticed the financial crisis.

頭のいい金持ちは気がついていましたが、彼らは金儲けのために収入が低い人たちを騙して儲けました。
Clever and wealthy people noticed the financial bubble, however, they deceived the lower income families.

「ちょっと待って、サブプライムローンって何？」
"Wait a second. What is subprime loan?".

アメリカでは1998年以降、土地がどんどん上がり続けました。
In America, land price had been rising since 1998.

その後、数年で２倍近くになったという物件も多いです。
In fact, a lot of land doubled in price within just a few years.

そこで、幾らかの金持ち人間が考えることは？
Then what do some wealthy people think?

「知識のない低収入の人たちを騙して儲ける。」です。
That would be, "Let's make a profit by deceiving non-dedicated and low-income people."

低収入の人たちでも知識があれば騙されませんが、アメリカで
は知識がないから低収入なんです。
If low-income people have financial knowledge, they
might not be tricked, however, many of them don't have
that financial knowledge, and that's why their incomes are
low.

アメリカも土地の金額はいろいろです。
Land values vary greatly in America.

ニューヨークやロスアンゼルスのような都市部は高いですが、
LAでも車で３０分も行けば、土地の値段は5分の１なんてとこ
ろもあります。
The housing prices in NY and LA are expensive, however,
there are many places that are 1/5 of the price if you
just drive 30 minutes.

都市部から車で二時間のところに行けば、不便で安いところも
たくさんあります。
If you drive about two hours from the inner city, there are
many inexpensive areas though they're certainly not as
convenient.

　お金のない人は、家を買えません。しかし、悪徳なセールスマ
ンはこう言います。
Low-income families can't buy houses. However, this is
what ill-intentioned salespeople say.

「ここは安い土地だけど、将来は二倍、三倍もの値段になる。
お金がなくても、ローン組んで買って将来家を売れば儲かるか
ら大丈夫！」
"The housing price here is inexpensive now, but it will
double or triple in the future. Even if you don't have

money, get a loan from the bank to purchase it and then just sell it in the future. Everything will be all right.

低所得者はこう思います。
Some lower-income families may think like this.

「こんな高金利のローンは確実に払えないけど、後で売ればいいや。」
"I definitely won't be able to pay such a high interest loan, but we can just sell it in the future."

銀行も、リスクが高いけど金利が高いので、喜んでそれを助長します。
Banks also want to be involved since they can get high interest income although the risk is high.

それを煽るように、今度はセールススタッフがこういうローン商品を作り始めます。
On top of that, sales staff start creating loan products like this.

「5年間は、支払い0です！今払えなくても大丈夫！頭金もいりません！ローンは5年後から始まります！」
"You don't need to pay interest for the first five years. It's totally fine that you don't pay anything now. You don't even need a down payment. The loan repayment will start in five years."

知識がない低所得者はこう思います。
Some low-income families without financial knowledge think like this.

「なんですって！！じゃあ、ローン払えなくても、5年後に家の値段が上がった時に売れば、ローンどころか金儲けできるじゃん！」
"Wow! That means we can sell the house in 5 years after the value has gone up and before we have to worry about repaying the loan!"

こうして、多くの低所得者はどんどん家を買います。
Likewise, many low-income families buy houses one after another.

そして、悪徳な金融関係者はそのローンを債権化して、金融商品にしました。
Then, bad financial agencies securitize the loan mortgage and make loan products.

簡単にいうと、ローンのお金の受け取りを売るんです。
To put it simply, they sell the right to receive housing loans.

だから、売った人はそこで終わり。
So the seller receives the money and that's it.

その債権を買った人は、将来ローンの受け取りをする。
The buyers of the loan mortgage security are supposed to receive the loan repayment in the future.

しかし、家のローンが払えない人がたくさんいたら？
However, what if there are many people who can't repay the housing loan?

これが「サブプライムローン」です。
This is called a "subprime loan".

もちろんそのサブプライムローンの債権を買った人は、お金を
受け取れないので、損をします。
Of course, the buyers who purchased the subprime loan
securities can't receive the money, so they lose their
money.

それを世界中の投資家が買ったため、問題はどんどん悪化して
いきます。
Many investors all over the world purchased these
housing loan mortgage securities, so the problem got
bigger and bigger.

どうして知識があるはずの投資家たちまでが騙されたのか？
How were so many supposedly knowledgeable investors
deceived?

ここまで聞いたら、中身空っぽの金融商品です。
These loan mortgage securities are financial products
which have no value.

どうしてかというと、大手格付け会社のムーディーズ、S&P,
Fitch、などが　このアホな商品の格付けを最高のAAAにしてい
たからです。
The reason why is that the large rating companies, such
as Moody's, S&P, or Fitch, rated these products with the
highest rank, AAA.

欲に駆られた金持ちは、よく中身を調べないで格付け会社を信
じます。
Those wealthy people trusted the rating companies
without looking at the details themselves, driven by their
greed.

そうして、うまいことその中身のない金融商品が売れていきました。
Then, the garbage financial products sold well.

S&P500のS&Pですよ？
It's S&P 500 Index's S&P.

信じるでしょう。
Of course, many people would trust such rating.

優秀なアナリストがいっぱいいるアメリカの大手格付け会社ですよ？？
Those are America's large rating companies that have a lot of elite analysts.

だけど、その嘘に気づくのはそんなに難しいこと？
But is it that difficult to find out the lie?

全然難しいことではありません。
It's not difficult at all.

なぜかというと、新聞に危険性は十分警告されていたんです。
It's because newspapers reported on enough financial crises to know.

私は2004年から、経験もなくアメリカにある日本の銀行で働き始めました。
I started working at a Japanese bank in America without any prior banking experience.

当時はアナリストではなく、ただのアシスタントです。
At the time, I was just an assistant, not an analyst.

でもラッキーでした。
However, I was lucky.

私の仕事は、ほぼ毎日8時間、LAタイムズ紙、ウォール・ストリート紙、日経新聞を読んで、アメリカに起こっていることで気がついたことをレポートにし、日本の本社に送ることでした。
My job was to read newspapers such as the LA Times and the Wall Street Journal every day for eight hours, and report what happened in America to the head office.

その仕事を2、3年くらいしました。
I continued the job for few years.

リーマンショックは、2008年に起こりましたよね？
Lehman Shock occurred in 2008, right?

私は2004年から2007年まで毎日、毎日、新聞をひたすら読んでいたんです。
I had read newspapers every day from 2004 to 2007.

住宅バブルがどのように形成されていくのかを学びました。
I learned how housing bubbles form.

そして、気がついたことは、新聞の1枚目の見出しには、「住宅の値段はこれからどんどん上がる！今がチャンス！」と、大きく楽観的なことが書かれ、中身にはその危険性がたくさん書かれているのです。
What I noticed was that the first page of every newspaper says something optimistic like, "The housing price is accelerating. Now is your chance to buy houses!", and then cautions about it are written inside of the newspapers.

低所得者は1枚目にしか気がつきません。
Many low-income families only notice the first page.

欲深い金持ちは、良い事しか見たくありません。
Greedy wealthy people want to see optimistic opinions only.

私の仕事は、それらをレポートにすることだったので、
　「この住宅ブームはバブルらしい。頭金なし、ローン払いは5年後、という危険なローンがいっぱい。」ということを書きました。
My job was to report those things, so I wrote, "This housing bubble might burst soon. There are many loans without down payments and five years postponed loan repayments".

それを提出すると、支店長に、「住宅バブルなわけないでしょう。」と言われました。
When I submitted the report, the general manager at the time said, "It can't be a housing bubble."

それでもとりあえず、そのレポートは本社に送られました。
Anyways, the report was sent to the head office.

すると、日本の本部からこういうメールをいただきました。
Then, we received this e-mail from the head office.

　「そちらにはいい従業員がいらっしゃるんですね。もっと詳しい内容を送ってもらえませんか？」
"You have such as skilled employee. Would you please send us more information?"

ちょっと自慢ぽくなりましたが、新聞を毎日読んでいれば誰でもわかることでも、欲深くなると内容が頭に入らない、というお話でした！
It sounds like I am showing off, however, my point is, if you are greedy, you can't see reality.

ちなみに、リーマンショックでお金が半分になった、という人はその時株を売ってしまった人
By the way, people who lost half of their money due to the Lehman Shock were people who sold their stocks then.

そのまま保有している人は、今お金は倍になっています。
People who held onto their stock then have now doubled their money.

皆さんも、優秀なアナリストを信じるのではなく、欲に惑わされず、現実を見つめながら、利益を増やしていきましょう！
So, everyone, don't blindly follow elite analysts' opinions driven by greed. Let's make a profit by looking at reality!

第16章 - S&Pインデックスファンドの保持者は勝ち組
CH16 - S&P Index Fund Owners Are Winners

S&P500インデックス株を持っている人ならわかると思うけど、去年2018年の年末あたりの評価損はすごかったですよね。
If you have S&P500 Index stocks, you know this. The unrealized loss last year at the end of 2018 was terrible, wasn't it?

2018年の11月から2019年の1月くらいにかけて、米国株はがくーん、と落ちましたね。
The price of U.S. stock plunged between November 2018 and January 2019.

その時にするべき行動は。。。
What should you do in times like those?

「落ちた時こそ優良株を買え。」です。
"Buy more good quality stocks when the prices drop".

以下のは私がFidelityに口座のある一部の単独株（とキャッシュ）ですが、図を見るとわかるように去年2018年9月には70,000ドル近くに行っていたのですが、落ちた時は55,000ドルくらいに下がっています。
The graph below is part of my individual stock account and some cash with Fidelity Investment Company. As you can see, the balance reached around $70,000 in September 2018, and dropped to $55,000 in Jan 2019.

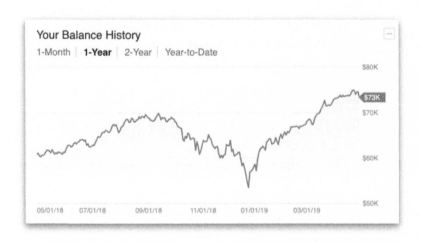

この口座には15,000ドルのキャッシュが含まれていたので、落ちていく過程でアップル株を8,000ドルくらい買いました。
This account included a cash amount of $15,000, so I purchased $10,000 of Apple stock.

当時アップル株を約5兆円分($50 billion)持っているウォーレン・バフェットは叩かれましたが、株価が回復している今は当時叩いた人からはコメントなし。
Warren Buffett who held about ¥5 trillion ($50 billion) of Apple stock was criticized when stock price plunged, however, now that the stock price has recovered, nobody talks about him anymore.

10,000ドルくらいで買ったアップル株は、今は17,000ドルくらいになりました。
That $10,000 of Apple stock increased to $17,000.

まあ、大した儲けじゃないですけど、基本的な戦略はこうしたほうがいいという例です。
Well, it's not ridiculously large profit, however, the basic strategy should be like this.

アップルは2018年9月は最高の一株230ドルくらいになりましたが、2019年1月は150ドルまで落ちました。
The stock price of Apple as of September 2018 reached $230, and then dropped to $150 as of January 2019.

でも今（2019年12月）は280ドルまで回復しています。
However, now (December 2019) it has returned to $280.

2006年にはアップル株は10ドルくらいでしたし、ウォーレンバフェットさんは痛くもかゆくもない上に、まだ上昇していくわけです。
Apple stock was only about $10 in 2006, so the price decline never hurt Warren Buffett, moreover, the stock price is still rising.

アップル株が10ドルの時に1万ドル分（約100万円）買っていたら、今は2,800万円です。
If you bought $10,000 (¥1million) of Apple stock when the price was $10, it would now be $280,000 (¥28.0million).

何が言いたいかというと、優良株なら落ちても株を信じて売らないこと。
My point is, if the stock is superior, even if the stock price declines every now and then, trust it and do not sell it.

そして落ちている時こそ、その優良株を買い占めること。
And when the price is down, you should buy a lot.

でも、そこでグッとこらえて、大きくジャンプ！
But if you are a little patient, it will surely make a big jump!

2019年6月にも落ちたけど、またもやジャンプ！
In June 2019, the stock price dropped again, but then it jumped back up!

こうやって、落ちては上がり、落ちては上がり、儲けていくんです。
As such, U.S. stock prices go up and down and we make profit.

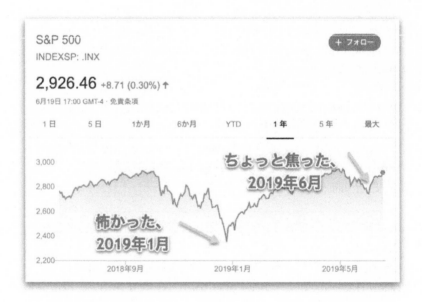

S&P 500 Index は上のような動きをしていましたが、私のIT株が多い個別株アカウントも同じような動きをしています。
The S&P 500 Index moved as above. One of my accounts which holds individual stocks moves as S&P 500 moves.

Your Balance History
1-Month | **1-Year** | 2-Year | Year-to-Date

うろたえるなという私も、7万ドルあったのが4ヶ月後の2019年1月に5万ドル近くになったのには焦りましたね。
Even me, who insists on being patient, was scared when the balance of $70,000 in January 2019 dropped to $50,000 in four months.

だけど、歯を食いしばってそのままにしとくんです。
However, you should leave it as it is.

というか、「見ないふり、見ないふり〜」という感じにします。
Well, it's more like, "I don't see it, I don't see it" (although I can see it).

私はアメリカの現在の経済力を信じているので、落ちてもほっときます。
Since I trust the American economy, I don't sell stocks even when the price drops.

トランプさんのTwitter発言で、アメリカの株が上下する、って
いうけれど、アメリカの経済は底力があるので、どちらにして
も下がって、上がって、を繰り返して上がります。
People say Mr. Trump's Twitter has an effect on American
stocks, however, the American economy is stable after all,
so it is always steadily increasing.

だから、「トランプの発言で株が上下するアメリカ株は危な
い」という意見は間違っていると思います。
So, the opinion of "American stock is risky since it moves
according to Mr. Trump's Twitter" is in my opinion, incorrect.

第17章 - 世界同時株安傾向とか言うけれど
CH17 - Worldwide Stock Price Drops?

最近、株が下がると、「世界同時株安傾向」という人もいます
よね。
Recently, when stock prices go down, some people say
"Stock prices are going to drop all over the world."

2019年6月3日付け、アメリカS&Pの過去1年の動きはこうで
す。
As of June 3, 2019, the movement of the S&P Index of
America in the past year is as follows

5年を見るとこう。
The price index of the past five years is below.

以下は過去50年、2008年末のリーマンショック含む。
Below is the index price of the past 50 years, including
the Lehman Shock at the end of 2008.

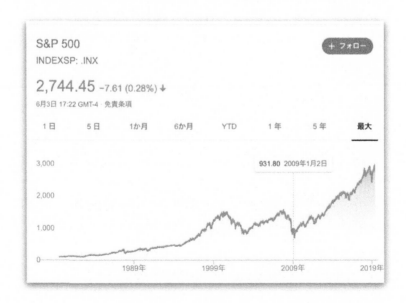

2008年末のリーマンショックが株安大ショック、なんて言いますが、株が下がる前の株価の今は2倍ですからね。
People say that the Lehman Shock dragged stock prices down to the bottom, though, the current stock price is double that of the highest stock price before Lehman Shock began.

下がった時に比べたら、3倍。
If you compare it to the lowest stock values of that time, the current stock price is triple that.

「そこで売っちゃう！？」って感じでしょう？
You'd think you would sell then, right?

世界経済はアメリカが引っ張っていって、同じ動きをすると言うけれど。。。
People say that America leads the world economy, so the worldwide stock price follows America's stock index, but...

日本の株の動きはと言うと？
How about Japan's stock prices?

一年は以下の通り。
Japan's stock index, Nikkei, for one year is as follows.

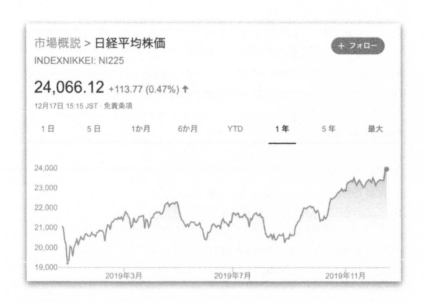

2019年10月くらいから良くなったきましたね。
It's moving up since Oct 2019.

5年は？
How about five years?

悪くないけど、不安定すぎるし、アメリカほどの伸びはない。
It's not bad but it's unstable, and it did not gradually go up like American stocks.

以下は最大30年です。
Below is for maximum 30 years.

30年前よりまだ下。
The current stock is lower than the stock index was 30 years ago.

日本の株の動きは悪いし、各々の決算書が良くても、アメリカの決算書がいい会社のようには伸びない。
Japan's stock price has not been doing well, and even if the each company's financial result was good, the company's individual stock price does not move up like American companies with similar financial results.

これはメキシコの株を買った時にも思いました。
I also thought this when I purchased Mexican stocks.

決算書がいいのに、アメリカの会社のようには伸びない。。。
Although the financial result was good, the individual
stock price does not go up like in America.

やっぱり国の力というのは大きいです。
After all, country's economic ability affects stock prices.

メキシコ政府は国の経済を活性化するために、10年以上前から
メキシコに車製造工場を作る日本の会社に無料で土地を与えた
り、返金不要の工場建築費を支払ったりして、日本の車会社、
またそれに伴うパーツ会社がこぞってメキシコに工場を作りま
した。
The Mexican government encouraged Japanese
automakers to build automobile plants in Mexico in order
to stimulate the economy more than 10 years ago. The
Mexican government offered free land and promised to
pay part of the expenses in building a plant. As a result,
Japanese automakers and parts suppliers built plants in
Mexico.

しかし、トランプ大統領がメキシコからアメリカへの車に追加
関税をかけると言う話が出るたびに、株価にも影響が出るし、
日本の車会社もメキシコに工場を作ることを敬遠したりします
よね。
However, every time President Trump suggests increasing
tariffs, the stock price drops and Japanese companies
become reluctant to build plants in Mexico.

メキシコ株は3年ほど前に買って、損はしていないものの値動き
が悪すぎてほぼ売りました。
I purchased Mexican stocks three years ago, however, the
stocks don't move as I expected, so I sold most of them.

でも、今後も株価の動きを見たいので、「Grupo
Aeroportuario」と言うメキシコの空港の会社だけは売ってい
ません。
However, I still have a Mexican stock of an airport
company called "Grupo Aeroportuario" since I would like
to observe the stock price movement.

決算書もとても良かったですし、需要もあるからと思いました
が、20万円程度なのですが、上がって、下がって、3年経って
もいまだに20万円くらいです。
The financial reports were great and there is demand, so I
purchased the stock amount for about ¥200,000 (about
$2000), however, it's still around $2000 three years later.

[GRUPO AEROPORTUARIO DEL SUREST SPON ADR 3yr]

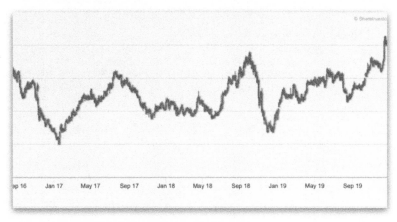

(2019年12月に２０％上がっていました。)
(It soared by 20% in December 2019.)

配当はしているので、時々何十ドルかお金が入っています。
Since the company pays out dividend, I occasionally
receive tens of dollars.

国の力はどうしようもないことを学びました。
I've learned I can't do anything about the country's
economic ability.

その中でも、メキシコ株という気持ちで、メキシコに支店をど
んどん拡大したアメリカの会社、ホームデポも買いました。
At the same time, I purchased American"Home Depot"
stock since they have expanded their business to Mexico.

ホームデポの株は3年前に9万円で買いましたが、今は18万円に
上がっています。なんでもっと買わなかったんだろう？
The stock price of Home Depot rose from ¥90,000
(about $900) to ¥180,000 (about $1800). I don't know
why I did not buy more of it.

やっぱりアメリカ経済は強い。。。
Yeah, the American economy is really strong…

決算書だけではどうにもならない壁があるということもあります。
There are always obstacles we can't overcome even
provided great financial results of individual companies.

第18章 - 年金・医療費・大学費用
CH18 - Pension / Medical Expenses / College Tuition

日本人の若者に、こんな質問を受けました。
I received this question from a young Japanese man.

いや、厳密にいうと、日本育ちの両親アメリカ人の若者からです。
Actually, he was a young American boy raised in Japan.

日本では、アメリカ国籍にするか、日本国籍にするか、２２歳までに選ばなければいけないルールになっています。
Before he turns 22 years old, he must choose between Japanese and American citizenship.

「僕は現在20なのですが、日本では僕らの世代は年金が貰えるかわからないと言われていますがアメリカではこのような問題は今のところないのでしょうか？」
"I am currently 20 years old. People say they are not sure if we receive national pension when we retire. Is there any problem like this in America?

私はこう答えました。
So I answered like this.

そもそもアメリカでも年金を期待していませんが、アメリカは経済世界一なので、年金をもらえる国としては一番期待できます。
Basically, many people don't expect enough pension to in America either, however, since America is economically the biggest country, the probability of pension is the highest.

アメリカ国民でも満額でもらえる年齢が折に触れて引き上げられ
ています。
In America, the age to receive pension in full occasionally
increases.

だから、アメリカではみんな将来のために株を買っています。
That's why people in America invest in stocks to be ready
for the future.

正社員だったら、ほとんどの会社が４０１kという株をサポート
しています。
Most companies provide investment support in the form
of a 401K to their full-time employees.

例えば、給料の中から$300株に入れたら、会社が$300払って
くれて合計$600が投資となります。
For example, if the employee invests $300 from their
paycheck, the employer can also contribute $300, a total
of $600 will be invested in the employee's account.

その株を何にするかは本人が決めますが基本mutual fund や
EFT（アメリカの株指標と同じように動く株のまとまり）です。
The employee decides which stock they choose, but
basically, you would choose a mutual fund or EFT.

しかもアメリカ経済は強いし、過去は結構な上がり方をしてい
るので、数1000万円レベルの儲けはそれほど驚くことではあり
ません。
On top of that, the U.S. economy has been strong and it
has really soared in the past, so it's not so surprising
even if the employee has made a few hundred thousand
dollars (￥10,000,000).

日本では株を買うことは一般的ではなく、年金だけをあてにしている若者が多くいます。これからは日本でももっと投資についての知識が広まればいいなあ、と思います。
In Japan, not everyone invests in stock, so many young people will rely on national pension. I hope they can gain some knowledge about investment in Japan.

最近では、金融庁が「年金だけでは足りない。投資をしよう。」と言うような趣旨のことを発表し、結構炎上していることもあるようです。
Recently Japan's financial agency announced that national pension by itself is not sustainable.

アメリカからすると、「え？当たり前じゃん？年金だけで足りると思ってたの？」と言う感じです。
When people in America hear that, many of them would probably say, "Huh? Of course it's not enough by itself."

アメリカでは、会社でも株のサポートがあり、働いていない人も入れるIRAという国が運営しているリタイアメントプランもあります。
In America, companies support employees' pension plans, and for many people there is pension plan called an IRA that is supported by the government.

日本でも似たようなものはありますが、会社で投資が当たり前、という風潮はありません。
There are similar pension plans in Japan as well, however, investment support from the company is not so common.

だからと言って、日本に住むのは不利なのか？
Even so, is it a disadvantage to live in Japan?

そんなことはありません。
Not at all.

アメリカは、医療費が異常に高いです。
In America, medical expenses are unbelievable high compared to Japan.

アメリカでは会社で雇用されていないで、まともな医療保険に自己負担で入ると月に約1,000ドル(10万円)します。
In America, if you are not employed and you want to get medical insurance to cover most expenses, the insurance premium would be about $1,000 per month.

会社ではその医療保険に当たる月1,000ドルを従業員のために負担しています。
Companies often pay about $1,000 for employees' medical insurance.

だから、起業しようと会社を辞めることはとてもリスクが高いです。
So it's risky to quit your full-time job and start a business.

保険が適用されない医療も多く、手術のために家を売った、という話も聞きます。
There are many medical expenses that insurance won't cover, so I sometimes hear about people selling their homes to pay for operations.

アメリカで10年以上働いていたら、老後にメディケアというものを使えますが、それを持っていても医療費の請求は怖いです。
If you work for more than 10 years in America, you will be eligible to receive Medicare operated by the government, but even then, the medical bill is scary.

例えば、私の両親はアメリカで10年働いてリタイヤしてしばらく住んでいたのですが、父が一度具合が悪くなって病院に一晩泊まりました。
For example, my parents worked in America for 10 years and retired, and then lived there for a while afterwards. Once my dad did not feel well so he stayed in a hospital overnight.

特に手術などが必要なくても病院に泊まってちょっと検査をするだけで、300万円（約30,000ドル）の医療費です。
The hospital charged $30,000 (about ¥3,000,000) although he did not get any operation.

その時のメディケアの規定では、入院の場合は20万円くらいが自己負担、外来の場合は医療費の20%負担です。
The medical plan at the time stated that the insurer would need to pay out of pocket $2,000 (¥200,000) for the inpatient fee, or the insurer has to pay 20% of the outpatient bill.

300万円の20%は、60万円ですよ！そんなこと日本でないですよね。
20% of ¥3,000,000 would be ¥600,000! This would never happen in Japan, right?

私がアメリカで出産した時は、娘はお腹の中でちょっとばい菌が入ってしまい、一週間入院しました。
When I delivered my daughter in America, my daughter got some kind of bacteria in my tummy, so the baby girl was hospitalized for a week.

その医療費は、なんと当時500万円。。。それは保険が全額カ
バーしましたが、保険がなかったら大変です。
The medical bill before insurance coverage was $50,000
(approx. ¥5,000,000). The medical insurance that my ex-
husband's company supported covered 100%, however, if
I did not have medical insurance, it would have been
tough.

アメリカでは、出産後病院には二日しか入院できないのです
が、看護師に「個室とグループ部屋、どちらがいいですか？」と
聞かれたので、「個室の部屋はいくらですか？」と聞いたら、
「保険が利かないので、一晩2,000ドル（20万円）です。」と
言われたので、「いいです、結構です！」と答えました。
In America, mothers who delivered a baby can stay only
for two days in the hospital. When I was hospitalized
after delivering my daughter, a nurse asked me, "Would
you like to stay in a private room or a group room?". I
asked, "How much is the private room for a night?", and
she said, "One night would be $2,000 (Approx. ¥200,000)
and the medical insurance does not cover that." So I said,
"No thank you!".

そのほか、保険があってもなぜか一回100ドル、200ドル払い
は結構普通です。
Other than that, even if the medical insurance covers it, I
often pay $100 to $200 out of pocket anyway.

私はアメリカでアメリカ国籍を取ったので、日本の国籍は喪失
しました。
I became an American citizen, so my Japanese
citizenship was revoked.

元日本人のアメリカ人として日本に住んでいて、ネットビジネスでドル収入を得ているのですが、日本の税務署に確認すると、ドル収入は納税不要と言われました。
I live in Japan as an American who used to be a Japanese citizen, and my income from my online business is paid in U.S. dollars. I confirmed with Japan's revenue office who told me that I don't need to pay tax in Japan since my income is paid in U.S. dollars.

収入はありませんが、在留カードは持っているので、日本の国民健康保険は受け取ることができます。
Although I don't have income in Japan, I have a resident card, so I am eligible to have national medical insurance.

その支払いが、毎月800円。なんて良い国なんでしょうか。
The monthly insurance premium is only ¥800 (approx. $8). What a nice country Japan is.

しかも、病院での自己負担は、毎回1,000円、2,000円。
On top of that, the out of pocket payment at my doctor's office is always about ¥1,000 ($10) or ¥2,000 ($20).

アメリカの大学の学費は、私立は1年500万円、州立は1年150万円。
The tuition of universities in America is as follows; private school tuition is about ¥5,000,000 ($50,000) a year, and public university tuition is about ¥1,500,000 ($15,000) a year.

日本は私立1年で計算すると約100万円、国立30万円。。
In Japan, private school tuition is about ¥1,000,000 ($10,000) a year and public university is about ¥300,000 (about $3,000) a year.

どう考えても、日本の学費は良心的としか思えない。。。
Without a doubt, tuition in Japan is reasonable.

日本に住んでいると、いいことがたくさんあります。
There are many advantages to living in Japan.

コンビニのトイレは綺麗だし、鍵を借りに行かなくていい。
The restrooms at convenience stores are clean, and we don't need to borrow the key from the casher.

うるさくないし、みんな親切。
It's not noisy, everyone is kind.

トイレに行くと、バックをかけるフックがある。
There is hooks to hang your bags in the restroom.

レストランにはバックを入れる箱がある！
There are boxes to put purses in at restaurants.

どこに行っても綺麗、食べ物やすくて美味しい、ヘアカットは上手だし、チップいらない。
Everywhere is clean, meals are inexpensive and delicious, haircuts are good, and we don't need to pay tips.

みんなお行儀がいい、順番守る！
Everyone has manners and no one cuts in line.

日本で働いていたらきっと大変だけど、脱サラした私には関係なし。
If I work at a corporation in Japan, probably it's stressful, though, since I work at home, it does not apply to me.

ということで、日本大好き〜！！
So, I love Japan!!

でも、株はアメリカ株を買います。
However, I buy American stocks.

私は日本語を外国人に教えて、日本で働ける外国人を育成して、日本の日経株価を上げることに協力しようと頑張っているんです〜。
I teach Japanese to non-Japanese and train non-Japanese to be able to work in Japan. I try my best to contribute to raise Nikkei stock index.

日本のいいとこ取りの私を怒らないで。
So please don't be upset that I get only advantages in Japan.

第19章 - 株投資はギャンブルか？
CH19 - Is Stock Investment a Gamble?

株投資はギャンブルかどうか？ いうと、
Is investing really a gamble?

リスクをどの程度とりたいか、によって、ギャンブルにすること
もできますが、守りたい金額は、安全に投資すればギャンブル
ではありません。
Depending on how much risk you can take, it could be
gamble, however, if you make low-risk investments, it
could not be gamble.

しかし、ギャンブルが悪いとも言いません。
I would not say gambling is bad, though.

守りたい財産はギャンブルにせず、遊びの部分を取り入れても良
い、ということです。
You keep the money you want to protect, and choose the
amount you want to gamble.

遊びを入れてギャンブルにする、と言っても、その分に関して
も、可能な限りの安全網を張り巡らせます。
Even if it's a gamble, you should try to lower the risk as
much as possible.

だから、自分の財産のうち、どれくらいの金額は守りたいの
か、と考える必要があります。
So, you should think about how much of your money you
want to keep for yourself.

リスクが高ければ高いほど、大きく儲かる可能性もあります
が、大きく損をする可能性もあります。
The higher the risk, the higher your chances of hitting it
big, but your chances of meeting a great loss will also
increase.

私は基本的には長期投資しかしません。
Basically, I only do long-term investment.

短期は、どう考えても安全網を張れないからです。
It's harder to lower the risk of short-term investment.

当たるときもあるかもしれませんが、落ちるときもあって安定
しませんよね？
You might get a lot of money, or you might lose a lot of
money. The higher the risk, the less stable.

安全に投資することは可能です。
It's possible to invest safely.

現在一番安全に投資、というのは、やはり世界第一位の経済大
国、アメリカのインデックス投資だと思います。
Currently the safest investment product is American
stock indexes such as S&P Index.

インデックス投資は、S&Pインデックスのように、アメリカの
全体の株の動きをするものです。
The stock price of index investment products moves as
the S&P Index moves.

証券会社がそれを商品として売っています。
Investment companies sell those index investments as
their products.

今は大きく動く株はグーグル、アマゾン、フェイスブック、アップルをまとめた名称のGAFAのようなIT系企業だと思います。
Recently the individual stocks which have been increasing significantly are IT industries such as Google, Amazon, Facebook, and Apple, collectively called "GAFA".

このS&Pインデックスは、食品、運輸、建築、様々な産業がまとまった株の指標になります。
The S&P Index includes a collection of major companies from various industries.

例えば、昔からあるマクドナルドなどは、安定していますが、大きく株があがるような予想はできません。
For example, the stock of company with its long history is stable, however, I can't imagine that the stock prices would soar suddenly.

だから、株の動きは大きくないものの、確実に利益を得ることはできます。
So the stock price movement is not huge, however, you will be able to profit for sure.

そのような株も入ったまとまりがS&Pインデックスファンドになります。
S&P Index funds include a collection of individual stocks like McDonald's.

そして、ギャンブルはどんな投資かというと、たとえばまだあまり評価されていないけれど、自分で探し出した会社、例えばGAFAに変わるようなこれから頭角を出してくるだろう、と思うIT株などです。

And if you ask me what kind of investment would be gambling, I guess it would be IT stock like GAFA, but a company who has yet to get any reputation or has not been noticed yet.

でもやはり、最低100万円くらいはかけないと、いくら１０倍になったとしても1000万円なので、10万円くらいかけたところで、、、という話でもあります。
However, you won't be able to make a big profit if you don't invest at least about $1,000,000.

個別株をいろいろ買って、利益を上げていく、という方法もありますが、その場合は、世界一の投資家、ウォーレンバフェットの年利２０％がいいところだと思ってください。
There is a way to make a profit by buying various individual stocks. In that case it's reasonable to think that the maximum annual return rate would be about 20% which is Warren Buffett's average annual return rate.

株に対して、あまりにも夢を見すぎている人たちがいます。
Some people dream too much about stocks.

世界一の投資家が２０％なのに、一般人がそれ以上行けると思いますか？
When the world's best investor's annual return is 20%, would you think ordinary people can get more than that?

一時的にはその年利を超えることができるかもしれませんが、何十年もそれを続けることは無理です。
It might be possible to get an annual return more than 20% temporarily, however, it's hard to maintain for more than a decade.

最終的な目的は、老後の足りないソーシャルセキュリティ年金を補うものが投資だとアメリカでは考えられています。
In America, generally people think the purpose of investment is to support themselves after retirement to cover what social security does not.

だけど、投資が年金のためだけだと何かつまらない。
However, if the investment is only for retirement, it's not so fun.

だから遊び枠を設けたい。
So some people want to invest a bit for fun.

ということで、その遊び枠は大きく当たるかもしれないけれど、大きく損することもある。
The fun part might hit big, or it might drop significantly.

だけど、できる限り、安全網を張り巡らせたい。
However, we would like to do it as safely as possible.

だから決算書を読めるようにならないといけない。
Therefore, we must be able to read financial statements.

そんな気持ちで投資について考えていってほしい、と思います。
I want you to think about investment in that way.

第20章 - 株で損する方法
CH20 - How to Lose Your Money Investing in Stocks

「投資で一日、何百万円稼いだ。」という話を聞いたから、
「自分も投資だ！」という方もいます。
When someone says, "I earned few hundred million yen
(about few ten thousand dollars) in a day", some people
respond with, "I will start investing too!".

ウォーレンバフェット並みの資産があれば、何百万円の儲けは
簡単ですが、そうでない場合は、堅実に投資をすることをオスス
スメします。
If you have as much asset as Warren Buffett, it's easy to
earn few hundred million yen (about few ten thousand
dollars) in a day, but if you don't, I recommend you invest
more carefully.

冷静に考えて、ウォーレンバフェットが年の勝率が２０％なの
に、私たちのような一般人が１０倍、１００倍にできるわけな
いじゃない？
Think about it, when the annual return rate is 20%,
average people like us can't get 1,000% or 10,000%
annual return.

いや、できると思うけど、問題は、「その勝率を10年以上続け
られるか？」ってことです。
Well, we may be able to do it, however, the problem is
maintaining that for 10 or more years.

１０倍、１００倍にしているってことは、それなりのリスクを取っているので、確率的には、次の年には、マイナス１０倍、１００倍になる、ということです。

If you get 1,000% or 10,000% annual return for the year, I am sure you took high risk, therefore, the probability is that it would be minus 1,000% or 10,000% for the next year.

じゃあ、私が目指しているところ、個別株で5年キープできている率はどこかというと、「２０％です。」

So, what is my target annual return and what annual return have I gotten in the past five years for individual stock investment? The answer is 20%.

だけど、「10年続けられる、リスクが少ない２０％です。」

However, it is "20% annual return that I can continue receiving for 10 years".

例えば、今年２０％、来年１０％、再来年３０％、、、という感じならOKです。

For example, if the annual rate was 20%, 10%, and 30% this year, next year and two years later, respectively, it's good.

何も勉強しないでリスクを取らずに投資をすると、年率は３％だと思います。

If you don't learn how to invest and do not take high risks, the annual return rate would be 3%, I think.

それを２０％にする方針でユーチューブチャンネルを始めました。

I started my YouTube channel to go from 3% annual return to 20%.

安全に、確実に、そこに近づける方法です。
It's a good way to reach an annual return of 20% safely
and effectively.

それでは、タイトル、「株で損する方法」について述べます
と、
Now, let me introduce to you how to lose your money
investing in stocks, as the chapter title says.

（1）時間軸が短すぎる。
(1) The time span is too short.

確実に資産を増やすには、長期投資です。
In order to increase your asset for sure, long-term
investment is recommended.

短期では、なかなかリスクを低くするのが難しい。
It's difficult to lower the risk if it's short-term investment.

成長株は、一時的に株価が落ちても必ず回復するので、弱った
時は見守ることです。
Price of rapidly growing stocks may drop occasionally,
but it will recover after that for sure, so when it's weak,
you should just be patient and wait.

例えていうなら？
For example?

えーっと、、
Well…

好きな女子に彼氏がいても、その二人がうまくいかなくなるのを年単位でじっと待ち、チャンスを狙ってその時アプローチ！
Let's say your love interest has a boyfriend already, be patient until they break up, and approach her when the time comes!

彼氏がいても、簡単に諦めるな。
Even if she has a boyfriend, do not give up.

いや、例がおかしいかな。
Well, this example is probably not right.

例えていうなら？
For example?

えーっと…
Well…

彼の企業が失敗して借金だらけになっていても、その才能を見抜いてじっとサポートし、彼が弱っている時にプロポーズするように誘導する！
Let's say your boyfriend's business completely fails and a lot of debt is leftover. You know he has superior talent though, so you support him while he is weak, and lead him to get married with you!

その後、ただ彼が大金持ちになるのを待つのみ！
Then, you just wait and see that he becomes a rich man.

えーっと、私はたとえ話が苦手なので、以上。
Well, I am not a good storyteller, so that' it for now.

（２）夢を見すぎる。
(2) You dream too big.

私には妹が二人いるのですが、一人の妹は専業主婦で「5万円投資するから、1000万円にできない？」と、言ってきました。
I have two younger sisters. One of them is a house maker. She said, "I will invest 50,000 yen (about $500), so can you turn that into 10,000,000 yen (about $100,000)?"

私は妹に「おバカさん、そんなわけないだろ。まずはパートを探して、毎月5万円投資しろ。」と言いました。
I said, "That's not possible, silly. First, find a part-time job and invest 50,000 yen ($500) a month".

（３）第六感で株を買う。
(3) You use your "sixth sense" to buy stocks.

決算書なども勉強しないで、感で株を買って儲かることもあるかもしれない。
You may be able to make a profit from investment using your sixth sense without learning how to read financial statements.

しかし、簡単にゲットしたものは、簡単にいなくなるんです。
However, if you go without effort, it will be gone quickly.

英語でいうと、「Easy come, easy go」です。
In English, it is "Easy come, easy go".

うまく言った時に調子に乗らない、うまくいかない時に取り乱さないことです。
Even when it goes well, don't be too excited. When it's not going so well, don't be too upset.

そんな精神的な安定感が大事です。
That kind of mental stability is important.

また、市場を間違えるといくら頑張っても無理なこともある。
Also, if you choose the wrong market, even if you put in a
lot of effort, most of time it's not going to end well.

日本の株価指標、日経インデックスの３０年間の動きはこうで
す。
Japanese stock index, Nikkei, moved for the past 30
years as follows.

アメリカの株指標、S&P500はこうです。
America's Stock Index, S&P 500 moved as follows.

市場概説 > S&P 500
INDEXSP: .INX

3,192.52 +1.07 (0.034%) ↑

12月17日 16:53 GMT-5 · 免責条項

| 1日 | 5日 | 1か月 | 6か月 | YTD | 1年 | 5年 | 最大 |

4,000
3,000
2,000
1,000
0

1985年　　1995年　　2005年　　2015年

これから日本には頑張って欲しいと思っていますが、このように市場を間違えると、とんでもなく損をします。
I am cheering on Japanese stock market, though, if you pick the wrong market, you will lose your money significantly quickly.

（４）自分の頭で考えない。
(4) You don't think for yourself.

アメリカの経済を２０年間見てきて、住宅バブル崩壊などの推移を見てきました。
I have looked at the American economy for about 20 years now, and saw how the housing bubble burst.

そして、ある金持ちは情報がない人たちを利用して金を儲け、経済というのは回っているんだなあと思いました。
And I thought the world economy comes and goes as certain wealthy people trick non-educated people to earn money.

そう言う金持ちに踊らされないようにするためには、知識が必要ですね。
If you don't want to be tricked by certain wealthy people, you should be educated.

損はしないとして、毎年３％の儲けなら何も考えずにS&P500のようなアメリカのインデックスファンドを買うといいと思います。
If you are satisfied with an annual return of 3%, I recommend you buy U.S. index funds such as S&P 500.

20%狙うなら、感で買うのはなく、勉強しましょう。
If you would like to aim for an annual return of 20%, let's learn how to buy stocks without using your sixth sense.

20%って小さいと思いますか？
Do you think an annual return of 20% is too low?

あと何年生きる？
How many more years are you living?

20%の年利は、決して小さくないですよ。
20% annual rate is never low.

年利20%を狙いませんか？
Don't you want to aim for an annual return of 20%?

第21章 - こうすれば儲かる米国株
CH21 - How to Make Profit on Investment

米国株の長期投資で儲ける方法は、ズバリ、「最初から株価が落ちることを見込んでいること」です。
How to make a profit from long-term U.S. stock investment is actually "to you assume the stock price will decline at some point."

よく不思議に思います。
I often wonder why.

「今日かなり株で損した」という人は、なんで自分の株が一番上の時と比べるんだろう？投資したときに比べると上がっているでしょう？と思います。
People might say, "Today I lost a lot of money by investing in stocks.", however, they actually mean the stock has declined today. In the end, they will still make a net profit.

安定した米国株でも、基本的には「上がって、下がって、上がって、下がって」を繰り返して上がっていきます。
Even stable U.S. individual stocks fluctuate very often but inevitably go up.

それを下がったからといって売っていたら、いつまでたっても株で儲けることはできません。
If you sell the stock when it goes down, you will not be able to profit from that stock.

株が下がった時に、比べるのは、「株を買った時の金額！」です。
When the stock prices decline, you should be comparing the current price to the price you initially purchased the stock at.

また、株価が上がったかどうかを判断するのに、一日単位で比べるのは問題外です。
When you consider if your stock price goes up or down, it's useless to see the price movement for just a single day.

１ヶ月単位も早すぎる。
One month is too easy as well.

一年ごとに何％上がったのかを確認する作業をしましょう。
Let's check the stock performance in one year.

信じた株を買ったわけだから、よっぽどのことがない限り、売らないことです。
You trusted the stock, that's why you bought it, so you should not sell it unless something unacceptable thing happens.

できれば10年は持って欲しいです。
If you can, I want you to wait 10 years.

最終目的は、「老後の足りない年金を補助するもの」と思うべきです。
The overall purpose is, "to invest in stocks to cover what pension doesn't."

時々使いたい時には、引き落とししてもいいです。
If you want to use the money, you can cash out
occasionally.

また起業して将来の儲けの種まきをしているなら、引き落とし
てもいいでしょう。
Also, if you are planting seeds for your future, such as
starting your own business, it's good to withdraw some
cash.

それは「自分」という株に投資しているんですから。
That means you are investing in "me" stock.

「自分」将来上がる株なの？どうなのよ？
Do you think "me" stock will grow?

「自分」がしているビジネスは、将来人々が欲しいサービス、
または商品なのか？
Do you think people will want to buy your services or
products in the future?

決算書を見る時に大事なことの一つですが、会社がコントロー
ルできない時代の波や、運もあります。
There is one thing that you have to keep in mind when
you read a financial statement. There are uncontrollable
incidents such as trends or luck.

そういう逆境に強いかどうか、というのもお金を貸すかどうか
の判断基準になります。
We judge if managements are mentally strong enough to
deal with those obstacles when we lend money.

それを、「管理職の逆境の時の対応能力があるかどうか」
と言う基準になります。
It's the base called, "manager's ability to deal
with adverse conditions".

調子のいい会社でも必ず悪い時が来るものです。
Even if the company is doing well now, surely something
bad will happen eventually.

そういう時に、どういう対応をできるのか？
Then, how will the management deal with it?

そこで勝ち組、負け組が決まります。
Likewise, the winner and loser will be determined.

「あなたは逆境に強いの？」
Are you capable of dealing with adverse conditions?

起業する人なら必ず考えて欲しいこと。
It's important if you want to start your own business.

女子が男子を選ぶ時にも考えて欲しいこと。
When a woman chooses a man, it's something that
should be considered.

そして、会社の株を買う人なら、そこを見て、悪い時期にも逆
境に負けない会社と判断したなら、そっと寄り添うことも大事
です。
Then, if you want to buy individual stocks, look at the
"ability to deal with adverse conditions", and if you
conclude that the company has enough ability to deal
with it, it's important to stay with the stock.

女子なら、今あるお金だけを見るのではなく、逆境に強い男子を選んで、弱った時にはちゃんとサポートできるかどうかを考えるのが大事です。

If you are woman, don't look at the money he has currently, but rather think about if you can support him when adverse conditions come about.

そのあと成功する男性になるんですから！

After dealing with it, he will be a successful man!

第22章 - Adobe株(ADBE)をチェック！
CH22 - Let's Take a Look at Adobe Stock (ADBE)!

日本語ユーチューブチャンネルは、3年前からやっているのですが、日本語なんで、登録者は全員外国人です。
I started my YouTube channel for Japanese learning three years ago. It's Japanese learning, so all the subscribers are non-Japanese.

最近米国株ユーチューブチャンネルを初めたのですが、初めて日本人の方からコメントをもらいました！
Recently I started another YouTube channel about U.S. stock investment and got comments from Japanese people for the first time!

「こんにちは。 米国株初心者でこちらで勉強させて頂いております。 流動比率が1.13で自己資本比率が49% の米国株ADBE の場合はどう考えれば良いのでしょうか？ 流動比率が1.5を超えていないけれど 自己資本比率は20%を超えている場合の評価判断について花子さんの見解をお聞きしたいです。」
"Hi. I have been learning about U.S. stock with you since I am a beginner investor. What do you think about the ADBE stock with current ratio 1.13x and equity ratio 49%? The current ratio has not exceeded 1.5x, but the equity ratio has exceeded 50%. In this case how would you evaluate this one?"

ということで、Adobe 2018/11 （珍しい11月決算期） １０
K(有価証券報告書）をチェックしてみました！
So, I checked the 10K (annual financial report) of Adobe
as of FYE 11/2018 (November fiscal year end is unusual).

	11/2018	11/2017
ASSETS		
Current assets:		
Cash and cash equivalents	$ 1,642,775	$ 2,306,072
Short-term investments	1,586,187	3,513,702
Trade receivables, net of allowances for doubtful accounts of $14,981 and $9,151, respectively	1,315,578	1,217,968
Prepaid expenses and other current assets	312,499	210,071
Total current assets	4,857,039	7,247,813
Property and equipment, net	1,075,072	936,976
Goodwill	10,581,048	5,821,561
Purchased and other intangibles, net	2,069,001	385,658
Other assets	186,522	143,548
Total assets	$ 18,768,682	$ 14,535,556
LIABILITIES AND STOCKHOLDERS' EQUITY		
Current liabilities:		
Trade payables	$ 186,258	$ 113,538
Accrued expenses	1,163,185	993,773
Income taxes payable	35,709	14,196
Deferred revenue	2,915,974	2,405,950
Total current liabilities	4,301,126	3,527,457
Long-term liabilities:		
Debt	4,124,800	1,881,421
Deferred revenue	137,630	88,592
Income taxes payable	644,101	173,088
Deferred income taxes	46,702	279,941
Other liabilities	152,209	125,188
Total liabilities	9,406,568	6,075,687

ふむふむ。。。
I see…

これ見ると分かりますが、11/2018は、Current Assetが
$7.2billion から＄4.8billionに減ってますよね？
You see that current asset decreased from $7.2 billion in
11/2017 to $4.8 billion in 11/2018.

なんでだと思いますか？
Why do you think this happened?

また、その下のGoodwillが＄5.8billionから＄10.5billionまで増
えていますよね？
Also, goodwill increased from $5.8 million to $10.5 billion.

Goodwillは会社を買収した時に増えます
Goodwill increases when the company acquires other companies.

なぜかというと、売った時に、簿記上の価値よりも高く売った分が高いので、その差額がGoodwillになります。
The reason why is because when the company purchased the business, the purchased value was higher than the book value, so the difference would be goodwill.

だから、会社の買収でお金が減った、と考えられます。
So we can guess that their cash decreased due to the acquisition.

では、キャッシュフローを見てみましょう。
Now, let's look at the cashflow.

CONSOLIDATED STATEMENTS OF CASH FLOWS

(In thousands)

	Years Ended		
	November 30, 2018	December 1, 2017	December 2, 2016
Cash flows from operating activities:			
Net income	$ 2,590,774	$ 1,693,954	$ 1,168,782
Adjustments to reconcile net income to net cash provided by operating activities:			
Depreciation, amortization and accretion	346,492	325,997	331,535
Stock-based compensation	609,562	454,672	349,297
Deferred income taxes	(468,936)	51,605	24,222
Unrealized losses (gains) on investments, net	793	(5,494)	3,145
Excess tax benefits from stock-based compensation	—	—	(75,105)
Other non-cash items	7,193	4,625	2,022
Changes in operating assets and liabilities, net of acquired assets and assumed liabilities:			
Trade receivables, net	(1,983)	(187,173)	(160,416)
Prepaid expenses and other current assets	(77,325)	28,040	(71,021)
Trade payables	54,920	(45,186)	(6,281)
Accrued expenses	43,837	151,164	65,591
Income taxes payable	479,184	(34,493)	43,115
Deferred revenue	444,693	475,402	524,840
Net cash provided by operating activities	4,829,304	2,912,833	2,199,728
Cash flows from investing activities:			
Purchases of short-term investments	(566,084)	(1,931,011)	(2,285,222)
Maturities of short-term investments	765,860	759,737	769,228
Proceeds from sales of short-term investments	1,709,186	1,393,929	860,849
Acquisitions, net of cash acquired	(6,314,382)	(459,626)	(48,427)
Purchases of property and equipment	(203,772)	(178,122)	(203,305)
Purchases of long-term investments, intangibles and other assets	(13,513)	(29,918)	(58,433)
Proceeds from sale of long-term investments and other assets	4,923	2,134	5,777
Net cash used for investing activities	(4,615,582)	(442,877)	(959,533)
Cash flows from financing activities:			
Purchases of treasury stock	(2,050,000)	(1,100,000)	(1,075,000)
Proceeds from issuance of treasury stock	90,990	158,351	145,697
Taxes paid related to net share settlement of equity awards	(393,193)	(240,126)	(236,400)
Excess tax benefits from stock-based compensation	—	—	75,105
Proceeds from debt issuance, net of costs	2,248,342	—	—
Repayment of capital lease obligations	(1,707)	(1,960)	(108)
Net cash used for financing activities	(5,568)	(1,183,735)	(1,090,706)
Effect of foreign currency exchange rates on cash and cash equivalents	(1,738)	8,516	(14,234)
Net increase (decrease) in cash and cash equivalents	(663,297)	1,294,757	134,755
Cash and cash equivalents at beginning of year	2,306,072	1,011,315	876,560
Cash and cash equivalents at end of year	$ 1,642,775	$ 2,306,072	$ 1,011,315
Supplemental disclosures:			
Cash paid for income taxes, net of refunds	$ 710,369	$ 396,668	$ 249,584
Cash paid for interest	$ 81,258	$ 69,430	$ 66,193
Non-cash investing activities:			
Investment in lease receivable applied to building purchase	$ —	$ 80,439	$ —
Issuance of common stock and stock awards assumed in business acquisitions	$ 2,784	$ 10,348	$ —

Acquisition（買収）で$6.3 billion払っています。
The company paid $6.3 billion in acquisitions.

ということで、メモでどこを買収したのか調べます。
So now let's search what the company acquired in the memo.

ACQUISITIONS

During fiscal 2018, we completed our acquisitions of Marketo, a privately held marketing cloud platform company, for $4.74 billion and Magento, a privately held commerce platform company, for $1.64 billion. As of the end of fiscal 2018, we are continuing to integrate Marketo and Magento into our Digital Experience reportable segment.

During fiscal 2017, we completed our acquisition of TubeMogul, a publicly held video advertising platform company, for $560.8 million. As of the end of fiscal 2018, we have integrated TubeMogul into our Digital Experience reportable segment.

We also completed other immaterial business acquisitions during the fiscal years presented.

See Note 2 of our Notes to Consolidated Financial Statements for pro forma financial information related to the Marketo acquisition. Pro forma information has not been presented for our other acquisitions during the fiscal years presented as the impact to our Consolidated Financial Statements was not material.

Subsequent to November 30, 2018, we acquired the remaining interest in Allegorithmic SAS ("Allegorithmic"), a privately held 3D editing and authoring software company for gaming and entertainment, for approximately $105.0 million in cash consideration. Allegorithmic will be integrated into our Digital Media reportable segment for financial reporting purposes in the first quarter of fiscal 2019.

See Note 2 of our Notes to Consolidated Financial Statements for further information regarding these acquisitions.

Marketo - $4.74 billion

Magento - $ 1.64 billion

合計で$6.3 billion ビンゴ〜！
In total, it's $6.3 billion Bingo!

それでは、買収後の１０Q（四半期）はどうなったでしょうか？
Now let's find out how their 10Q (quarterly financial result) was.

	Three Months Ended	
	March 1, 2019	March 2, 2018
Revenue:		
Subscription	$ 2,304,967	$ 1,793,358
Product	170,554	171,608
Services and support	125,425	113,981
Total revenue	2,600,946	2,078,947
Cost of revenue:		
Subscription	288,031	164,685
Product	12,105	12,877
Services and support	97,150	81,340
Total cost of revenue	397,286	258,902
Gross profit	2,203,660	1,820,045
Operating expenses:		
Research and development	464,637	348,769
Sales and marketing	781,518	580,957
General and administrative	216,109	170,440
Amortization of purchased intangibles	46,566	17,146
Total operating expenses	1,508,830	1,117,312
Operating income	694,830	702,733
Non-operating income (expense):		
Interest and other income (expense), net	4,266	16,672
Interest expense	(40,593)	(19,899)
Investment gains (losses), net	43,831	2,996
Total non-operating income (expense), net	7,504	(231)
Income before income taxes	702,334	702,502
Provision for income taxes	28,093	119,426
Net income	$ 674,241	$ 583,076
Basic net income per share	$ 1.38	$ 1.18
Shares used to compute basic net income per share	488,056	492,061
Diluted net income per share	$ 1.36	$ 1.17
Shares used to compute diluted net income per share	494,188	499,433

See accompanying notes to condensed consolidated financial statements.

悪くないですね。
It's not bad.

流動比率はどうなったか？
What happened to the current ratio?

	March 1, 2019 (Unaudited)	November 30, 2018 (*)
ASSETS		
Current assets:		
Cash and cash equivalents	$ 1,738,846	$ 1,642,775
Short-term investments	1,487,411	1,586,187
Trade receivables, net of allowances for doubtful accounts of $14,639 and $14,981, respectively	1,342,343	1,315,578
Prepaid expenses and other current assets	565,115	312,499
Total current assets	5,133,715	4,857,039
Property and equipment, net	1,104,065	1,075,072
Goodwill	10,707,715	10,581,048
Purchased and other intangibles, net	2,017,103	2,069,001
Other assets	542,938	186,522
Total assets	$ 19,505,536	$ 18,768,682
LIABILITIES AND STOCKHOLDERS' EQUITY		
Current liabilities:		
Trade payables	$ 145,292	$ 186,258
Accrued expenses	1,167,429	1,163,185
Debt	892,754	—
Income taxes payable	24,422	35,709
Deferred revenue	3,063,839	2,915,974
Total current liabilities	5,313,736	4,301,126
Long-term liabilities:		
Debt	3,236,833	4,124,800
Deferred revenue	134,353	137,630
Income taxes payable	655,036	644,101
Deferred income taxes	125,660	46,702
Other liabilities	168,433	152,209
Total liabilities	9,634,051	9,406,568
Stockholders' equity:		
Preferred stock, $0.0001 par value; 2,000 shares authorized; none issued	—	—
Common stock, $0.0001 par value; 900,000 shares authorized; 600,834 shares issued; 488,504 and 487,663 shares outstanding, respectively	61	61
Additional paid-in-capital	5,857,440	5,685,337
Retained earnings	12,579,311	11,815,597
Accumulated other comprehensive income (loss)	(150,432)	(148,130)
Treasury stock, at cost (112,330 and 113,171 shares, respectively), net of reissuances	(8,414,895)	(7,990,751)
Total stockholders' equity	9,871,485	9,362,114
Total liabilities and stockholders' equity	$ 19,505,536	$ 18,768,682

買収の影響で、流動負債の方が資産より多くなっていますね。
Current liability is larger than current asset due to the acquisition.

しかし、買収によって流動比率が悪いけれど、利益率は非常に良いです。
Although the current ratio is not good, the profitability is very good.

ADOBE INC.

CONSOLIDATED STATEMENTS OF INCOME

(In thousands, except per share data)

		Years Ended		
		November 30, 2018	December 1, 2017	December 2, 2016
Revenue:				
Subscription	$	7,922,152	$ 6,133,869	$ 4,584,833
Product		622,153	706,767	800,498
Services and support		485,703	460,869	469,099
Total revenue		9,030,008	7,301,505	5,854,430
Cost of revenue:				
Subscription		807,221	623,048	461,860
Product		46,009	57,082	68,917
Services and support		341,769	330,361	289,131
Total cost of revenue		1,194,999	1,010,491	819,908
Gross profit		7,835,009	6,291,014	5,034,522
Operating expenses:				
Research and development		1,537,812	1,224,059	975,987
Sales and marketing		2,620,829	2,197,592	1,910,197
General and administrative		744,898	624,706	576,202
Amortization of purchased intangibles		91,101	76,562	78,534
Total operating expenses		4,994,640	4,122,919	3,540,920
Operating income		2,840,369	2,168,095	1,493,602
Non-operating income (expense):				
Interest and other income (expense), net		39,536	36,395	13,548
Interest expense		(89,242)	(74,402)	(70,442)
Investment gains (losses), net		3,213	7,553	(1,570)
Total non-operating income (expense), net		(46,493)	(30,454)	(58,464)
Income before income taxes		2,793,876	2,137,641	1,435,138
Provision for income taxes		203,102	443,687	266,356
Net income	$	2,590,774	$ 1,693,954	$ 1,168,782
Basic net income per share	$	5.28	$ 3.43	$ 2.35
Shares used to compute basic net income per share		490,564	493,632	498,345
Diluted net income per share	$	5.20	$ 3.38	$ 2.32
Shares used to compute diluted net income per share		497,843	501,123	504,299

ビジネススタイルが、今の時代にぴったりです。
The business style matches the current business trend.

今は、Subscriptionビジネス、月額でもらうタイプ、が時代の
波だと思います。
I think subscription business in which the business owner
receives subscription fees monthly is a great modern
business structure.

155

基本的に在庫を抱えないでいいビジネスだから、研究費が高い
にしてもリスクが小さいです。
Basically, the business does not need to carry inventory.
Although the research & development fee is high, the
risk is low.

しかし、Adobeは今後大きくするための投資を行なっていま
す。
However, Adobe invests to expand business even further.

株の動きは？(調べたのは2019年5月23日)
How about stock movement?(researched on 5/23/2019)

11月に買収して、11月決算期の発表あたりにかなり落ちていま
すが、IT関連全般この時期落ちましたから、買収も関係あるの
かちょっといまわかりません。
The company acquired other companies in November
and the stock price dropped when the financial results

were announced, so I don't know now if the stock decline is related to the acquisition.

損益計算書の結果は良かったですね。
The result of income statement was good.

Adobe株の動きを最大期間で見てみましょう。
Let's take a look at the stock price movement in the maximum period.

20ドルくらいの時にかっとけば良かったね！
We should have bought the stock when the price was around $20!

ということで、そもそものビジネススタイルがいいので、流動比率が悪くても、自己資本率もかなり高いので、来年の2020年あたりも有望なんではないかと思います。

The business model is great, although the current ratio is not so good, the equity ratio is very high, so I think the Adobe stock will be doing good next year in 2020.

というか、私もこの株買いたい！
I mean I want to buy this stock!

ただ、来年なんかあって下がっても怒らないでくださいね。
However, don't be upset if the stock price declines next year due to some unforeseen event.

あと、買収した先の情報をもうちょっと調べた方がいいかも。
And I recommend that you collect more info about the company that Adobe acquired.

10年持っていたら、必ず結構儲かるということは言えます。
If you hold onto the stock more than 10 years, I am sure you will make a profit.

素敵な株のご紹介ありがとうございました！
Thank you for introducing this nice stock to me!

第23章 - マクドナルド株とチポトレ株
CH23 - McDonald's (MCD) and Chipotle (CMG) Stock

IT株の話が多かったので、今回はファーストフード系でいきたいと思います。
I have talked about IT stocks a lot, so now I would like to talk about fast food stocks.

アメリカのファーストフード株ですが、みなさんはどういう株の買い方をしたらいいと思いますか？
It is about fast food stocks in America. How do you think we should go about buying these?

まず、リスクを考えると、マクドナルドはリスクは低く、安定しています。
When we think about the risk, McDonald's is a stable and low-risk stock.

しかし、それで儲けようとなると。。。
However, if you want to make a lot of profit…

リスクが低いものは、安定している分、儲けも緩やかです。
The risk is low, but at the same time, the profitability is low since it's so stable.

まず、株の動きを見てみましょう。(2019年5月29日調べ)
First, let's take a look at the stock price movement (Researched on May 29, 2019).

1年の動きから見てみましょう。
Let's look at the price movement in the most recent month.

思ったよりはいいですね。
It's better than I thought.

次は5年の動き
Next, how about the price movement in five years.

あれ、これも思ったよりはいいですね。
Well, it's better than I thought as well.

5年で2倍です。
The stock price doubled in five years.

一番長いのでみてみましょう。
Let's see the longest one now.

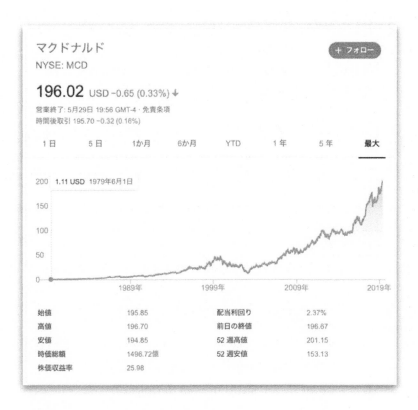

まあまあですね。1970年代は1ドルくらいだったので、その時買っていれば２００倍です。
It's all right. The stock price was about $1 in 1970's, so if you purchased it then, it is now 200 times higher.

私もマクドナルドはちょっと持っていますが、ちょこちょこ配当金が気がつかずに支払われています。
I have a little bit McDonald's stock, so I receive the dividend without really noticing.

最近は配当金が出る会社もなかなかないんですよね。
There are not so many companies which payout dividends.

だから、リスクが低いところで配当金をもらうというのも一つです。
So one idea is to buy stock of a company which is low-risk, and receive dividend.

それでは、私がどんなファーストフード店の株を持っているかというと、、、
Now I'll tell you which fast food companies' stocks I have.

3年くらい前にチポトレ やソニック株を買いました。
3 years ago, I bought Chipotle and Sonic stocks.

チポトレはメキシコ料理、ブリトーやタコスのファーストフード店です。
Chipotle is a Mexican fast food restaurant that sells burritos or tacos.

ソニックは、ハンバーガーでした（買収されました）。
Sonic is a hamburger shop (It was acquired).

買った理由は、もちろん「おいしいから」です！
The reason why I bought those is, of course because it is "delicious"!

そして、それほど知名度がなかったからです。
And it was not that famous.

が、ソニックは大手のファーストフード会社に買収されて、去年私の株は全部キャッシュで戻されました。
However, Sonic was acquired by a large size fast food company last year, so the stock was automatically returned, and it was cashed out.

買ったのは1株20ドルで、40ドルくらいで戻されたので儲けは出ています。
I purchased the stock when it was $20, and it was cashed out when it was $40, so I got a net profit.

このように、大手に買収された場合は大体結構いい値段で現金を受け取れます。
Likewise, when a company is acquired by large size corporation, you will receive with great deal.

日本ではあまり聞かない名前でしょうか？
You don't really hear about this restaurant in Japan, do you?

ソニックは、ロスから車でグランドキャニオンに行く途中で、暗くなるから早く何か食べないと、というところで車を駐車場に駐めながらそのままオーダーができました。駐車する場所ごとに、オーダーする機械があったのです。

Sonic was located on the way to the Grand Canyon from Los Angeles by car, and we had to eat before it got dark. Sonic was so convenient since we could park our car, order food from the car, and eat in the car while parked there. Each parking lot had a machine to order food.

それが素晴らしいと思った上に、味も美味しかったので、グランドキャニオンから帰ってすぐに買いました。
I thought it's wonderful, and on the top of that, it was tasty, so I bought the stock right after I returned to home from grand canyon.

オクラホマの会社だったので、まだロスでは見かけなかったんです。

Sonic was originally from Oklahoma, so I had not seen the restaurant before.

そして、チポトレですが、チポトレの3年の株の動きを見てみましょう。(2019年5月29日調べ)

And now let me talk about Chipotle. Before that, let's take a look at the stock price movement of Chipotle in the past three years. (Researched on May 29, 2019).

3年前の400ドルくらいの時に買ったので、儲けは十分出ていますが、マクドナルドの5年に比べると、安定はしていないですね。
I purchased the stock when the price was around $400 three years ago, so I got enough profit. However, the stock price movement has not been stable comparing with the one of McDonald's in the past five years.

最近も食中毒関係の何かで株が下がったと思います。去年は結構下まで落ちていたんですね。
I think the stock price dropped recently because of the food poisoning problem. The stock price kept dropping last year (2018).

しかし、こういう時が買い時ではあります。
However, that the time to purchase stocks.

ということで、今日のまとめとしては、有名ではない会社だと大きく儲かる可能性もあるが、安定はしていない。
So, as a conclusion for today, if you bought a stock which was not famous, you might be able to earn profit, however, it's not stable.

いい会社だと、買収されることもあるが、大抵結構いい儲けでキャッシュで支払われる。
If it was great company, there is a case that the company is acquired

安定路線で行きたいなら、マクドナルドなどにして、配当金をもらうという手もある。
If you want to invest without risk, you may be want to buy McDonald's stock and receive dividend.

しかし、大きな株の動きはないことが多い。

However, in many cases the stock price would not move significantly.

第24章 - IT株「GAFA」株価比較
CH24 - IT stocks "GAFA" Stock Price Comparison

ここ数年で株で儲けやすかったのは、やっぱりIT株のGAFA（グーグル・アマゾン・フェイスブック・アップル）です。
The stocks with the easiest profit in the last few years have all been "GAFA" (Google/Amazon/Facebook/Apple).

私はフェイスブック以外のGAFA株を3年以上持っていますが、一番儲かっているのはアマゾンです。
I have held GAFA stocks for more than 3 years with the exception of Facebook, and Amazon is the best performing stock.

2年半前の2017年1月ごろと今との差も見てみましょう。
Let's see the difference between the stock prices around January 2017 and current prices.

まずは、S&P500インデックスを見てみます。
First, let's take a look at the S&P 500 Index.

2019年6月12日現在は、2,879ドル、2017年初めは2,200ド
ルくらい、３１％の上昇率です。
June12, 2019, the stock price was about $2,200, and the
current price is $2,879. That's a 31% increase.

まあ、悪くないですよね。
Well, it's not so bad.

S&P500インデックスファンドなどは、リスクが少ないのでオ
ススメです。
The S&P500 Index fund is a good investment since the
risk is low.

それでは、グーグル株ですが、アルファベットという会社名でユ
ーチューブも持っています。
Now let's take a look at Google stock. Actually, the
company's name is "Alphabet", and they also own
YouTube.

Alphabet Inc Class A
NASDAQ: GOOGL

1,079.10 USD −1.94 (0.18%) ↓

営業終了: 6月12日 17:30 GMT-4 · 免責条項
時間後取引 1,079.10 0.00 (0.00%)

| 1日 | 5日 | 1か月 | 6か月 | YTD | 1年 | **5年** | 最大 |

792.45 USD 2016年12月30日

2019年6月付は1,079ドル、2017年初めは792ドル、上昇率
は、３６％。
As of June 2019, the stock price is $1,079, however, it
was $792 at the beginning of 2017. That's a 36% jump.

S&P500よりちょっと多いくらいです。
This price increase is a bit higher than S&P 500.

次に、アマゾンを見てみましょう。
Next, let's take a look at Amazon stock.

2019年6月付は1,855ドル、2年半前は760ドル、上昇率は
114%！
As of June 2019, it's $1,855, though, it was $760 two
years ago. That is a 144% increase!

これは結構稼ぎ頭です。
This one is great performer.

ちなみに、アマゾンは250ドルの時に買ったものもあります。
By the way, I purchased part of my Amazon stocks when
it was only $250.

次にフェイスブックです。
Next is Facebook..

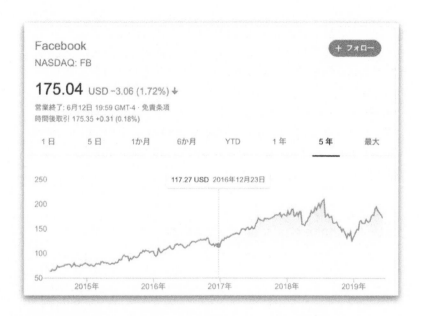

Facebook
NASDAQ: FB

175.04 USD −3.06 (1.72%) ↓

営業終了: 6月12日 19:59 GMT-4 · 免責条項
時間後取引 175.35 +0.31 (0.18%)

| 1 日 | 5 日 | 1か月 | 6か月 | YTD | 1 年 | **5 年** | 最大 |

117.27 USD 2016年12月23日

2015年　2016年　2017年　2018年　2019年

2019年6月付は175ドル、2年半前117ドル、上昇率は４９.
５％。悪くない、けど持っていない。
As of June 2019, the stock price is $175, and it was
$117 two years ago. It has increased by 49.5%. It's not
too bad, but I don't have Facebook stock.

なぜかというと、フェイスブック、個人的にあんまり好きじゃ
ないんです。。。
The reason why I don't have Facebook stock is that I
personally don't like Facebook….

ネズミ講式に、どんどん繋がりが広がっていく感じが好きじゃ
ない。
I don't like the way that the network is expanded like a
pyramid scheme.

でも今19歳のアメリカ生まれアメリカ育ちの娘もフェイスブックで自撮りをしたりして忙しそうだったので、みんな楽しくやっているのも分かりますが、ビジネス向きじゃなかったな〜という。
However, my 19 years old daughter who was born and raised in America is always busy taking selfies, and I know many people enjoy doing it, but I don't think it's for business.

それではアップルです。
Now, let's take a look at Apple stock.

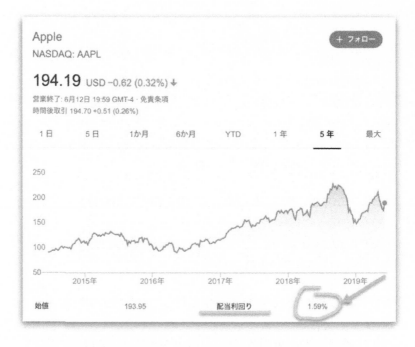

2019年6月付は194ドル、2年半前に115ドル、上昇率は69％！悪くないですね〜。
As of June 2019, it's $194, and was $115 two years ago. It increased by 69%! It's not bad at all!

しかも、気がついてなかったけど、GAFAの中で唯一配当があった！
On top of that, I did not realize that Apple is the only company which payout dividend.

私も今までフルタイムの仕事で忙しかったのもあるんですが、気がついたらアカウントにお金が入ってて、「あれ、どっか配当あったっけ？」ということがあります。
I had been too busy with my full time job to take time to check my own portfolio. I sometimes notice I got money on my investment account and think like, "Huh? Did I get dividend payout? Which company did it?".

これからはちゃんと見ないと。
I have to take a look at it carefully going forward.

アップル株を一年で見ると、(2019年6月12日時点)
Let's take a look at Apple stock price for a year (as of 6/12/2019).

190ドルが194ドル。ほぼ上がっていません。
It was $190 a year ago, and now it's $194. It leveled off.

最近アップルに５兆円持っている世界一の投資家ウォーレンバフ
ェットが叩かれていますが、2年半で見ると、７０％ですよ。
Recently, the world's best investor Warren Buffett who
holds more than $50 billion ($70 billion as of Dec 2019)
in Apple stock was publicly criticized, however, the stock
price of Apple has gone up 70% from the price it was
two years ago.

S&P500の2年の上昇率は３１％です。アップル株は、完全に勝
ち組です。
S&P 500 index rose by 31% in the past two years, so
Apple stock is a winner for sure.

基本的な考え方として、S&P500の上昇率を上回る個別株を保有している人は勝ち組です。
The basic acknowledgement is that if an individual stock price increases is higher than one of the S&P 500 stocks, the individual stock holder is a winner.

個別株はリスクなので、S&P500などのインデックスファンドを買うんですから。
People buy S&P 500 Index funds since individual stocks are riskier to hold.

というわけで、一年単位で上昇率は見た方がいいですが、5年くらいのスパンでも見て欲しいと思います。
In conclusion, it's better to check the stock price trend over the span of a year, but I also recommend you check the price over five years as well.

第25章 - (1) 1000万円分のグーグル株を買うか？
CH25 - (1) Should I Buy $100,000 of Google Stock?

グーグルはユーチューブも持っていますが、会社の名前は
Alphabetです。
Google owns YouTube. The Company's name is actually
Alphabet.

まず、上場したアメリカの会社の決算書を見るときはフルで全部
見たい場合は、「１０K」をグーグルします。
First of all, when you look for the financial statements in
full, you Google "10K".

ヤフーファイナンスなどでも決算書を見ることができますが、そ
れはハイライトだけが載っています。１０Kは決算期末の決算書
なので、100-200ページくらいあります。
You can find financial statements on "Yahoo Finance"
online, however, it's only a highlighted version of financial
statements. 10K is an annual financial reporting, so it
contains around 100-200 pages of financial reporting.

四半期は、「１０Q」です。
The quarterly report is called "10Q".

基本的そこに含まれているものは、以下の通りです。
Its contents are as follows.

(1) Consolidated Balance Sheet (連結貸借対照表)

(2) Consolidated Income Statement (損益計算書)

(3) Consolidated Cash Flow (キャッシュフロー)

それ以外にもどんな会社を買収した、とかこれからのビジネス計画などが他のページにあるので、パラパラと見るといいと思います。
Other than those, there are memos indicating their business plans, so I recommend you skim those.

でも正直、私も今まではめんどくさいと思って、10K全部を読んでいません。
But to be honest, I don't read the whole 10K.

でも、利回りは世界一の投資家、ウォーレンバフェット並みには勝っていて、損したことはありません。
However, my annual return is almost the same as Warren Buffett's, so I have never lost my money.

彼はどれくらいの年利だと思いますか？２０％くらいですよ。
What do you think his annual return is? It's about 20%.

それだけ？って思う？
Do you think, "That's it?"

アップルだけでも５兆円越え（2019年12月現在は７兆円）しているから、２０％ってすごいですよ。
His Apple stock already exceeds $50 billion ($70 billion as of Dec 2019), so 20% annual return is very good.

1000万円でも、２０％だったら一年に200万円の利益です。
If you have $100,000 in stock, you would get a $20,000 annual return.

私もやっぱり1,000万円くらいを一つの会社に払うなら、もう
ちょっと慎重に見ると思います。
If I buy $100,000 of a company's stocks, I would be more
careful.

というか、このブログを始めたのも、書いたらちゃんと調べる
から自分のためにも書いています。
Actually, I started my U.S. stock investment blog because
it would allow me to analyze companies more seriously.

基本的にめんどくさがりなので。
Basically, I am lazy.

株が上がる要因の多くは、（２）の損益計算書の最終利益の結
果です。
A stock price jump is often caused by the net income of
(2) Income Statement.

だけど、私が一番重要視しているのは、（１）の貸借対照表で
す。
However, what I think is most important is, (1) Balance
Sheet.

特に、
Especially,

（１）Current Ratio（流動比率）

（２）Equity Ratio （資本比率）

は、重要です。
are important.

ここを抑えれば、まあ危ないことはないでしょう。
If you check it, it probably won't go so badly.

英語で言うバランスシートだから、バランスが取れているかどうか、です。
It's "balance sheet" in English, whether it is balanced or not.

流動比率は、流動資産（現金、貯金、在庫など。すぐに現金にできるもの）÷ 流動負債（一年以内に払わないといけないもの）ですが１.５以上は欲しいです。
Current ratio is calculated by "Current Asset (thing that can quickly be converted to cash such as savings or inventories)" divided by, "Current Liabilities (debts matured within a year)". I think it should be more than 1.5x.

自己資本比率は、自己資本 / 総資産 x１００ です。
The formula of equity ratio is, Equity / Total Asset x 100.

２０％以上が好ましいですね。
More than 20% is preferable.

グーグル（アルファベット）を見てみましょう。
Now let's take a look at Google (Alphabet).

Alphabet Inc.
CONSOLIDATED BALANCE SHEETS
(In millions, except share amounts which are reflected in thousands, and par value per share amounts)

	As of December 31, 2017	As of December 31, 2018
Assets		
Current assets:		
Cash and cash equivalents	$ 10,715	$ 16,701
Marketable securities	91,156	92,439
Total cash, cash equivalents, and marketable securities	101,871	109,140
Accounts receivable, net of allowance of $674 and $729	18,336	20,838
Income taxes receivable, net	369	355
Inventory	749	1,107
Other current assets	2,983	4,236
Total current assets	124,308	135,676
Non-marketable investments	7,813	13,859
Deferred income taxes	680	737
Property and equipment, net	42,383	59,719
Intangible assets, net	2,692	2,220
Goodwill	16,747	17,888
Other non-current assets	2,672	2,693
Total assets	$ 197,295	$ 232,792
Liabilities and Stockholders' Equity		
Current liabilities:		
Accounts payable	$ 3,137	$ 4,378
Accrued compensation and benefits	4,581	6,839
Accrued expenses and other current liabilities	10,177	16,958
Accrued revenue share	3,975	4,592
Deferred revenue	1,432	1,784
Income taxes payable, net	881	69
Total current liabilities	24,183	34,620
Long-term debt	3,969	4,012
Deferred revenue, non-current	340	396
Income taxes payable, non-current	12,812	11,327
Deferred income taxes	430	1,264
Other long-term liabilities	3,059	3,545
Total liabilities	44,793	55,164
Commitments and Contingencies (Note 9)		
Stockholders' equity:		
Convertible preferred stock, $0.001 par value per share, 100,000 shares authorized; no shares issued and outstanding	0	0
Class A and Class B common stock, and Class C capital stock and additional paid-in capital, $0.001 par value per share: 15,000,000 shares authorized (Class A 9,000,000, Class B 3,000,000, Class C 3,000,000); 694,783 (Class A 298,470, Class B 46,972, Class C 349,341) and 695,556 (Class A 299,242, Class B 46,636, Class C 349,678) shares issued and outstanding	40,247	45,049
Accumulated other comprehensive loss	(992)	(2,306)
Retained earnings	113,247	134,885
Total stockholders' equity	152,502	177,628
Total liabilities and stockholders' equity	$ 197,295	$ 232,792

いや、素晴らしいですね〜〜。
Well, this is wonderful!

これ見ただけで、1000万円払いたくなりますね〜。
This makes me want to buy $100,000 in Google stock right now.

今は$17,000くらい持っていますが、112.5%アップしています。2年前に$8,000くらい買いました。
Currently, I have Google stock (Alphabet) in the amount of about $17,000, which is 50% higher than the price I

purchased it for. I bought $8,000 worth of stock two years ago.

Alphabet Inc.
CONSOLIDATED STATEMENTS OF INCOME
(In millions, except per share amounts)

	Year Ended December 31		
	2016	2017	2018
Revenues	$ 90,272	$ 110,855	$ 136,819
Costs and expenses:			
Cost of revenues	35,138	45,583	59,549
Research and development	13,948	16,625	21,419
Sales and marketing	10,485	12,893	16,333
General and administrative	6,985	6,872	8,126
European Commission fines	0	2,736	5,071
Total costs and expenses	66,556	84,709	110,498
Income from operations	23,716	26,146	26,321
Other income (expense), net	434	1,047	8,592
Income before income taxes	24,150	27,193	34,913
Provision for income taxes	4,672	14,531	4,177
Net income	$ 19,478	$ 12,662	$ 30,736
Basic net income per share of Class A and B common stock and Class C capital stock	$ 28.32	$ 18.27	$ 44.22
Diluted net income per share of Class A and B common stock and Class C capital stock	$ 27.85	$ 18.00	$ 43.70

See accompanying notes.

次の章で、どうしてグーグル株がいいか説明します。
I will explain why I think Google stock is a "must buy".

自分でも考えてみてください。
Please think about it yourself as well.

第26章 - (2) 1000万円分のグーグル株を買うか？
CH26 - (2) Should I buy $100,000 of Google Stock?

ところで、基本の貸借対照表はわかりますか？
By the way, do you know what a balance sheet looks like?

貸借対照表 (Balance Sheet)

資産 (Asset)	負債 (Liability)
	自 己 資 本 (Equity)

負債と自己資本を合わせたものが資産になります。
If you add liabilities and equity, you get total asset.

貸借対照表 (Balance Sheet)

資産 (Assets)	負債 (Liabilities)
流動資産(Current Asset) 50 固定資産(Non-Current Asset)50	流動負債(Current Liabilities)30 固定負債(Non-Current Liabilities)40 70
100	自己資本(Equity) 資本金(Capital)10 利益剰余金 (Retained Earning)20 30

（1）資産（Asset)

資産には流動（すぐにお金になるもの）と固定（すぐにはお金
にならないもの）があります。
There is current asset (easily converted into cash) and
non-current asset (not easily converted into cash).

（2）負債 (Liability)

負債にも流動（一年以内に払うもの）と固定（一年以上払わな
くていいもの）があります。
Liabilities also include current liabilities (debts which have
to be paid within a year) and non-current or fixed assets
(debts which do not have to be paid within a year).

（3）自己資本 (Equity)

返さなくていいもの。最初に会社を作った時のお金と、毎年積
み上がった利益。損が出たら減っていきます。
ここがマイナスならお話になりません。
You don't need to pay for equity. It's the money by which
the company was formed and the profit the company has
made in the past. If the company posted a loss, it would
be accumulated here. If the equity itself is negative, we
should not consider buying this stock.

それで、資産＝負債＋自己資本　になるはずなのです。
So, total asset should be total liabilities + equity.

写真によると、資本１００＝負債５０＋自己資本５０
According to the picture above, total asset 100 = total
liabilities 50 + equity 50.

はい、分かりましたか？（高校生に話すように書いています。大人の方だったらすみません。

All right, did you understand that? (I am talking like I am teaching a high school class. I know you are an adult, I'm sorry.)

それでは、昨日のアルファベットFYE12/2018の決算書のおさらいです。

Now, let's review the financial statement of Alphabet as of FYE 12/2018.

（１）流動比率はいくら？

(1) What is the current ratio?

（２）資本比率は、何パーセント？

(2) What percentage is equity ratio?

Alphabet Inc.
CONSOLIDATED BALANCE SHEETS
(In millions, except share amounts which are reflected in thousands, and par value per share amounts)

	As of December 31, 2017	As of December 31, 2018
Assets		
Current assets:		
Cash and cash equivalents	$ 10,715	$ 16,701
Marketable securities	91,156	92,439
Total cash, cash equivalents, and marketable securities	101,871	109,140
Accounts receivable, net of allowance of $674 and $729	18,336	20,838
Income taxes receivable, net	369	355
Inventory	749	1,107
Other current assets	2,983	4,236
Total current assets	124,308	135,676
Non-marketable investments	7,813	13,859
Deferred income taxes	680	737
Property and equipment, net	42,383	59,719
Intangible assets, net	2,692	2,220
Goodwill	16,747	17,888
Other non-current assets	2,672	2,693
Total assets	$ 197,295	$ 232,792
Liabilities and Stockholders' Equity		
Current liabilities:		
Accounts payable	$ 3,137	$ 4,378
Accrued compensation and benefits	4,581	6,839
Accrued expenses and other current liabilities	10,177	16,958
Accrued revenue share	3,975	4,592
Deferred revenue	1,432	1,784
Income taxes payable, net	881	69
Total current liabilities	24,183	34,620
Long-term debt	3,969	4,012
Deferred revenue, non-current	340	396
Income taxes payable, non-current	12,812	11,327
Deferred income taxes	430	1,264
Other long-term liabilities	3,059	3,545
Total liabilities	44,793	55,164
Commitments and Contingencies (Note 9)		
Stockholders' equity:		
Convertible preferred stock, $0.001 par value per share, 100,000 shares authorized; no shares issued and outstanding	0	0
Class A and Class B common stock, and Class C capital stock and additional paid-in capital, $0.001 par value per share: 15,000,000 shares authorized (Class A 9,000,000, Class B 3,000,000, Class C 3,000,000); 694,783 (Class A 298,470, Class B 46,972, Class C 349,341) and 695,556 (Class A 299,242, Class B 46,636, Class C 349,678) shares issued and outstanding	40,247	45,049
Accumulated other comprehensive loss	(992)	(2,306)
Retained earnings	113,247	134,885
Total stockholders' equity	152,502	177,628
Total liabilities and stockholders' equity	$ 197,295	$ 232,792

（１）流動比率 (Current Ratio)

Current Asset / Current Liability
135,676 / 34,620 = 3.9X

昨日なんて言ったか、覚えていますか？
Do you remember what I said?

「1.5以上が好ましい」
I said, "More than 1.5x is preferable."

めちゃくちゃいいですよ！3.9x！
The result of 3.9x is fantastic!

（2）自己資本率 (Equity Ratio)

Stock Holder's Equity / Asset
177,628 / 232,792 x 100
= 76.3%!!

なんて言いました？
What did I say?

「20%以上が好ましい」です。
I said, "More than 20% is preferable."

めちゃくちゃいいですよ！76.3%!
It's great that the result is 76.3%!

次回はもっと深く見て行きます。
In the next chapter, we will take a look at their financial results in depth.

第27章 - (3) 1000万円分のグーグル株を買うか？
CH27 - (3) Should I Buy $100,000 of Google Stock?

今回は、３回目です。
This is third one.

ささっと、損益計算書、貸借対照表を確認したので、キャッシュフローも見てみましょう。
We have already checked the Statement of Income and Balance Sheet, so let's take a look at Cashflow this time.

実際、ここまで貸借対照表がいいと、キャッシュフローは見なくてもいいことは分かります。
Actually, since the balance sheet is very good, sometimes it's not necessary to check the Cashflow.

キャッシュ（現金）フローですから、キャッシュの流れを見るわけで、資産の現金に$16 billion あることがわかります。
It's "Cashflow" so we are going to see the flow of cash. Since the Balance sheet shows the cash of $16 billion under Asset, so they have cash.

一応見ましょう。
Let's take a look just in case.

	Year Ended December 31,		
	2016	2017	2018
Operating activities			
Net income	$ 19,478	$ 12,662	$ 30,736
Adjustments:			
Depreciation and impairment of property and equipment	5,267	6,103	8,164
Amortization and impairment of intangible assets	877	812	871
Stock-based compensation expense	6,703	7,679	9,353
Deferred income taxes	(38)	258	778
(Gain) loss on debt and equity securities, net	73	37	(6,650)
Other	376	294	(189)
Changes in assets and liabilities, net of effects of acquisitions:			
Accounts receivable	(2,578)	(3,768)	(2,169)
Income taxes, net	3,125	8,211	(2,251)
Other assets	312	(2,164)	(1,207)
Accounts payable	110	731	1,067
Accrued expenses and other liabilities	1,515	4,891	8,614
Accrued revenue share	593	955	483
Deferred revenue	223	390	371
Net cash provided by operating activities	36,036	37,091	47,971
Investing activities			
Purchases of property and equipment	(10,212)	(13,184)	(25,139)
Proceeds from disposals of property and equipment	240	99	98
Purchases of marketable securities	(84,509)	(92,195)	(50,158)
Maturities and sales of marketable securities	66,895	73,959	48,507
Purchases of non-marketable investments	(1,109)	(1,745)	(2,073)
Maturities and sales of non-marketable investments	494	533	1,752
Cash collateral related to securities lending	(2,428)	0	0
Investments in reverse repurchase agreements	450	0	0
Acquisitions, net of cash acquired, and purchases of intangible assets	(986)	(287)	(1,491)
Proceeds from collection of notes receivable	0	1,419	0
Net cash used in investing activities	(31,165)	(31,401)	(28,504)
Financing activities			
Net payments related to stock-based award activities	(3,304)	(4,166)	(4,993)
Repurchases of capital stock	(3,693)	(4,846)	(9,075)
Proceeds from issuance of debt, net of costs	8,729	4,291	6,766
Repayments of debt	(10,064)	(4,377)	(6,827)
Proceeds from sale of subsidiary shares	0	800	950
Net cash used in financing activities	(8,332)	(8,298)	(13,179)
Effect of exchange rate changes on cash and cash equivalents	(170)	405	(302)
Net increase (decrease) in cash and cash equivalents	(3,631)	(2,203)	5,986
Cash and cash equivalents at beginning of period	16,549	12,918	10,715
Cash and cash equivalents at end of period	$ 12,918	$ 10,715	$ 16,701
Supplemental disclosures of cash flow information			
Cash paid for taxes, net of refunds	$ 1,643	$ 6,191	$ 5,671
Cash paid for interest, net of amounts capitalized	$ 84	$ 84	$ 69

See accompanying notes.

普通は、営業からのキャッシュフローと投資からのキャッシュ
フローを足してプラスだったらいいかなという感じです。
The basic idea is that if the free cashflow from operating
activity plus investing activity is positive, the condition is
deemed good.

営業活動によるキャッシュフローは、営業からできた現金です。
Cashflows from operating activity show the cash derived from operation.

投資活動からのキャッシュフローは、投資からの現金だから、土地を買えば減るし、投資したら減ります。
Cashflows from investing activity show the cash derived from investing activities, so if the company purchases land or invests, the cash decreases.

財務活動からのキャッシュフローは、お金を借りれば増えるし、返せば減ります。
Cashflows from financing activities show the cash derived from financing activities, so if the company borrows money, the cash increases and if it pays back the loan, it will decrease.

全部合わせて調整した現金が$16.7 billion 。ここは、貸借対照表の現金と合うはず。
All of the cash from the three activities above amounts to $16.7 billion. This number should match the cash under the balance sheet.

合わなければ、会計士は合うまでお家に帰れません。
The accountant who creates the financial statements can't go home until it matches.

Alphabet Inc.
CONSOLIDATED BALANCE SHEETS
(In millions, except share amounts which are reflected in thousands, and par value per share amounts)

	As of December 31, 2017	As of December 31, 2018
Assets		
Current assets:		
Cash and cash equivalents	$ 10,715	$ 16,701
Marketable securities	91,156	92,439
Total cash, cash equivalents, and marketable securities	101,871	109,14
Accounts receivable, net of allowance of $674 and $729	18,336	20,838
Income taxes receivable, net	369	355
Inventory	749	1,107
Other current assets	2,983	4,236
Total current assets	124,308	135,676
Non-marketable investments	7,813	13,859
Deferred income taxes	680	737
Property and equipment, net	42,383	59,719
Intangible assets, net	2,692	2,220
Goodwill	16,747	17,888
Other non-current assets	2,672	2,693
Total assets	$ 197,295	$ 232,792
Liabilities and Stockholders' Equity		
Current liabilities:		
Accounts payable	$ 3,137	$ 4,378
Accrued compensation and benefits	4,581	6,839
Accrued expenses and other current liabilities	10,177	16,958
Accrued revenue share	3,975	4,592
Deferred revenue	1,432	1,784
Income taxes payable, net	881	69
Total current liabilities	24,183	34,620
Long-term debt	3,969	4,012
Deferred revenue, non-current	340	396
Income taxes payable, non-current	12,812	11,327
Deferred income taxes	430	1,264
Other long-term liabilities	3,059	3,545
Total liabilities	44,793	55,164
Commitments and Contingencies (Note 9)		
Stockholders' equity:		
Convertible preferred stock, $0.001 par value per share, 100,000 shares authorized; no shares issued and outstanding	0	0
Class A and Class B common stock, and Class C capital stock and additional paid-in capital, $0.001 par value per share: 15,000,000 shares authorized (Class A 9,000,000, Class B 3,000,000, Class C 3,000,000); 694,783 (Class A 298,470, Class B 46,972, Class C 349,341) and 695,556 (Class A 299,242, Class B 46,636, Class C 349,678) shares issued and outstanding	40,247	45,049
Accumulated other comprehensive loss	(992)	(2,306)
Retained earnings	113,247	134,885
Total stockholders' equity	152,502	177,628
Total liabilities and stockholders' equity	$ 197,295	$ 232,792

だから現金がこんなにあって、昨日行った色々な数字が良ければ、キャッシュフローはいいはず。
So if the balance sheet cash is high enough, and if the other indexes show great numbers, we can estimate that the cashflow statement should be great too.

ところで、$16.7 billionって何円？
By the way, how much yen is $16.7 billion?

	日本語	英語
1	1 円	0.01 USD (= 1 cent)
2	10 円	0.1 USD (= 10 cents)
3	100 円	1 USD
4	1,000 円	10 USD
5	1 万円	100 USD
6	10 万円	1 thousand USD (= 1K USD)
7	100 万円	10 thousand USD (= 10K USD)
8	1,000 万円	100 thousand USD (= 100K USD)
9	1 億円	1 million USD (= 1M USD)
10	10 億円	10 million USD (= 10M USD)
11	100 億円	100 million USD (= 100M USD)
12	1,000 億円	1 billion USD (= 1B USD)
13	1 兆円	10 billion USD (= 10B USD)
14	10 兆円	100 billion USD (= 100B USD)
15	100 兆円	1 trillion USD (= 1T USD)

1.67兆円くらいです。
It's about 1.67 cho-yen.

わーお！
Wow!

でもウォーレンバフェットは、アップルだけで５兆円の株を持っているしね。(2019年12月付では7兆円)
But Warren Buffett holds about $50 billion in just Apple stock. ($70 billion as of 12/2019)

第28章 - (4) 1000万円分のグーグル株を買うか？
CH28 - (4) Should I Buy $100,000 of Google Stock?

決算書をチェックしましたが、ちょっと疲れたので、とりあえずグーグルの株価の動きをもう一度見てみましょう。
We've checked financial statements, now we are exhausted, so let's take a look at the stock price movement of Google (Alphabet).

まずは１ヶ月から。(2019年5月8日付)
First let's check the stock price over the past month. (as of 5/8/2019)

第一四半期は3年ぶりの低い伸びで株価下落。
The financial result of 1Q was the lowest it's been in the last three years, so the stock price dropped.

こういう時が株を買うチャンスなんですよね〜。
This is your chance to buy the stock.

あとで第一四半期の決算書を調べてみたいと思います。
We'll check the financial statements as of first quarter.

四半期の決算書はなんというでしょうか？
What is first quarter financial result called?

はい、10Qです。
Yes, it's called 10Q.

1年で見ると、1月にドーンと落ちましたね。
When we look at the stock price, it took a hit in January.

この時はこぞってIT関係株が落ちました。
At the time most IT-related stocks dropped.

こんなのは全然大丈夫です。
But don't worry at all.

買い時だったのは、見てすぐ分かりますよね。
You can see that it was a good time to buy.

5年で見ると、半分以下、500ドルくらいでした。
When we look at the chart of the past five years, it was
once about $500, half the price it is now.

私は確か、2016年くらいに買ったと思います。
I think I bought the stock around 2016.

Alphabet Inc Class A
NASDAQ: GOOGL

1,182.25 USD +3.39 (0.29%) ↑

5月8日 11:06 GMT-4 · 免責条項

| 1日 | 5日 | 1か月 | 6か月 | YTD | 1年 | 5年 | **最大** |

2004年は54ドルです。
It was $54 in 2004.

この時、その時働いていた会社のITスタッフが、「グーグルって
いう検索エンジンはいい」と言っていました。
At the time, IT staff at a company I worked said, "The
search engine called Google is wonderful.".

そんな時代だったんですねー。
That kind of year it was.

まだ娘が5歳でフルタイムで働いていたので、株とか見る時間な
かったです。
At the time, my daughter was only five years old and I
already had a full time job, so I did not have time to check
stock prices.

その年から銀行で働き始めました。
I started working at a bank then.

グーグルは、今は大きく伸びる前にユーチューバーを片付け始めていますね。
I think Google is trying to clean up YouTubers before the Company expand.

月に何百万円も払っていたユーチューバーへの広告収入を突然ストップしたり、顔を出さずにスクロールする動画には支払うのをやめたりしています。
Google started not to pay affiliate fee to YouTubers who used to receive few million yen a month, or they stopped paying to YouTubers who scroll the screen and don't show their faces .

来年から５Ｇが始まって、ライブ動画が止まらなくなったり、動画の時代が本当に到来するのでその準備だと思われます。
I think real YouTube video era is coming next year along with 5G, so that live streaming would not stop.

私のビジネスも、有料会員へのライブ配信なので、相当助かります。
My business relies on the live streaming, so 5G would help my business a lot.

だから、私はグーグル株に今いくら払うべきか調べているところです。
So I am considering how much Google stock I should buy now.

次の章では、株価が落ちた原因の第一四半期決算署について調べます。
For next chapter, we will look for the reason why the stock price dropped due to the 1Q financial result.

第29章 - (5) 1000万円分のグーグル株を買うか？
CH29 - (5) Should I Buy $100,000 of Google Stock?

まずは、株価が下がった第一四半期 アルファベット2019年3月を見てみましょう。
First, let's look at Alphabet's first quarter from March of 2019 in which the stock price dropped.

株が下がる理由は、最終の儲けが減ったからですよね。
The reason for this drop was because their profit went down.

「Revenue」 が売上で、損益計算書を見ればわかります。
You can see the company's revenue by looking at their statement of income.

「Net Income」 が最終収益です。

Alphabet Inc.
CONSOLIDATED STATEMENTS OF INCOME
(in millions, except per share amounts; unaudited)

	Three Months Ended March 31,	
	2018	2019
Revenues	$ 31,146	$ 36,339
Costs and expenses:		
Cost of revenues	13,467	16,012
Research and development	5,039	6,029
Sales and marketing	3,604	3,905
General and administrative	1,403	2,088
European Commission fine	0	1,697
Total costs and expenses	23,513	29,731
Income from operations	7,633	6,608
Other income (expense), net	2,910	1,538
Income before income taxes	10,543	8,146
Provision for income taxes	1,142	1,489
Net income	$ 9,401	$ 6,657
Basic net income per share of Class A and B common stock and Class C capital stock	$ 13.53	$ 9.58
Diluted net income per share of Class A and B common stock and Class C capital stock	$ 13.33	$ 9.50

See accompanying notes.

日本語訳をつけてみます。
Let me add Japanese translation.

Alphabet Inc.
CONSOLIDATED STATEMENTS OF INCOME
(in millions, except per share amounts; unaudited)

	Three Months Ended March 31,	
	2018	2019
Revenues 売上	$ 31,146	$ 36,339
Costs and expenses: 経費		
Cost of revenues 売上原価	13,467	16,012
Research and development 研究開発費	5,039	6,029
Sales and marketing 宣伝費	3,604	3,905
General and administrative 一般管理費	1,403	2,088
European Commission fine ヨーロッパコミッション罰金	0	1,697
Total costs and expenses	23,513	29,731
Income from operations	7,633	6,608
Other income (expense), net その他収入	2,910	1,538
Income before income taxes	10,543	8,146
Provision for income taxes 税金予想	1,142	1,489
Net income	$ 9,401	$ 6,657

売上は上がっていますが、粗利益はどうでしょうか？
The sales rose, but how about the gross margin?

3/2018: 13,467 / 31,146 = 43.2%
3/2019: 16,012 / 38,339 = 41.76%

まあ下がったけどそれほどでもない。
It decreased, but not by that much.

あ、ヨーロッパ、コミッション罰金がありましたね！
Oh, there is a European commission fine!

あと、研究開発費も高くなっています。
Also, the research & development is high.

これは将来に向けていいことかもしれませんよね。
It might be good for the company's future.

一般管理費も、まあ増えますよね。
Selling general and administrative expenses would increase.

その他収入がやけに減っている。。なんだったんだろう？
 Other income dropped significantly though… What was it?

こうやって、先に数字を見て、どんなことがあったのかをこの決算書の補足説明やニュースで調べます。
Likewise, we should check the numbers on the financial statements and find out what happened by reading the supplementary memos of financial statements or news.

でも、損はでていなくて、去年と比べて落ちたというだけです。
However, there are no real losses, the revenue just went down a bit from last year.

だから、バランスシートも悪くなりません。
So, the balance sheet isn't awful.

Alphabet Inc.
CONSOLIDATED BALANCE SHEETS
(in millions, except share amounts which are reflected in thousands, and par value per share amounts)

	As of December 31, 2018	As of March 31, 2019 (unaudited)
Assets		
Current assets:		
Cash and cash equivalents	$ 16,701	$ 19,148
Marketable securities	92,439	94,340
Total cash, cash equivalents, and marketable securities	109,140	113,488
Accounts receivable, net of allowance of $729 and $761	20,838	19,149
Income taxes receivable, net	355	111
Inventory	1,107	1,053
Other current assets	4,236	4,406
Total current assets	135,676	138,207
Non-marketable investments	13,859	14,474
Deferred income taxes	737	750
Property and equipment, net	59,719	60,528
Operating lease assets	0	8,837
Intangible assets, net	2,220	2,063
Goodwill	17,888	17,943
Other non-current assets	2,693	2,547
Total assets	$ 232,792	$ 245,349
Liabilities and Stockholders' Equity		
Current liabilities:		
Accounts payable	$ 4,378	$ 3,710
Accrued compensation and benefits	6,839	5,072
Accrued expenses and other current liabilities	16,958	19,382
Accrued revenue share	4,592	4,318
Deferred revenue	1,784	1,667
Income taxes payable, net	69	761
Total current liabilities	34,620	34,910
Long-term debt	4,012	4,066
Deferred revenue, non-current	396	391
Income taxes payable, non-current	11,327	11,605
Deferred income taxes	1,264	1,282
Operating lease liabilities	0	8,206
Other long-term liabilities	3,545	1,417
Total liabilities	55,164	61,877
Commitments and Contingencies (Note 10)		
Stockholders' equity:		
Convertible preferred stock, $0.001 par value per share, 100,000 shares authorized; no shares issued and outstanding	0	0
Class A and Class B common stock, and Class C capital stock and additional paid-in capital, $0.001 par value per share: 15,000,000 shares authorized (Class A 9,000,000, Class B 3,000,000, Class C 3,000,000); 695,556 (Class A 299,242, Class B 46,636, Class C 349,678) and 694,782 (Class A 299,444, Class B 46,527, Class C 348,811) shares issued and outstanding	45,049	46,532
Accumulated other comprehensive loss	(2,306)	(1,780)
Retained earnings	134,885	138,720
Total stockholders' equity	177,628	183,472
Total liabilities and stockholders' equity	$ 232,792	$ 245,349

See accompanying notes.

自己資本率がちょっと減りましたが、７０％台はキープしています。

The equity ratio went down a bit, but it's still keeping 70%.

自己資本率＝stockholder's equity / Total Asset
= 183,472 / 245,349 = 74.7%

以前も言いましたが、私はバランスシート（貸借対照表）を見ます。
I have said it before, but I always look at balance sheets.

なぜでしょうか？
Why would that be?

儲けが下がったとしても、理由によっては今後大きくジャンプする予兆だったりもします。
Even if the revenue decreases, you can determine whether or not it will jump back up again depending on the reasons why it went down initially.

そんな時に、みんなが「儲けが下がった」という理由で株を売ったら、そこで安い値段で株を買えばいいですよね。
At times like those, everyone sells their stock because "the profit went down", but actually, you should be buying stock instead.

株で安定して儲けている人はみんなこれを知っています。
Everyone who earns a stable income from stocks knows this.

だけど、決算書を見ないでニュースで株を買う人は踊らされ、損をして、「もう二度と株は買うか。」ということになります。
However, people who do not read financial statements and just buy stocks based on news may suffer big losses and decide not to invest in the stock market again.

私も株で損したことはありませんが、簡単だと思いませんか？
I haven't lost money in the stock market, but don't you think it's easy?

第30章 - (6) 1000万円分のグーグル株を買うか？
CH30 - (6) Should I Buy $100,000 of Google Stock?

決算書はチェックして、バランスシート（貸借対照表）がいいことは確認しました。
We've checked the financial statements and confirmed that the balance sheet looks good.

売り上げもよし、儲けもよし。
The sales and net income look good as well.

買うとして、他に有利な点は何でしょうか。
If you buy it, what else is good about Google (Alphabet)?

アルファベットはいろんな部門ありますが、グーグルの広告収入が売り上げ全体の85%です。
Alphabet has various divisions though income from Google's advertisement accounts for 85% of total sales.

ですから、他の部門はあまり考えないことにします。
Therefore, I don't consider the other divisions very much.

グーグルは今年になって、ブログのアフィリエイトで稼げないようにいろんな設定を始めるし、独自の方法でルール違反していたり、ただの勘違いだったりで、稼いでいるユーチューバーの広告収入を一方的に打ち切りにしたりしています。
Google rolled out a major algorithmic update that affects search results in significant ways, so many bloggers who earn a lot of revenue from affiliate fees lost their source of income. Also, Google has demonetized some YouTubers who don't follow the terms of service, but also

demonetized other YouTubers due to an error in the system.

これから伸びる前にいろんな整理をしているようにも見えます。
It seems that Google is restructuring YouTube before the business expands.

不安な要素としては、あまりにも力を持ちすぎていることです。
The concern is that Google has too much influence.

考えてみてください。
Think about it.

私たち日本人は、（あ、わたしはアメリカ人だった）日々の生活にどれくらいアメリカの会社に関わっていますか？
We Japanese (Oh, actually I am an American), are involved with American companies on a daily basis.

多くの人は、ユーチューブ毎日見るでしょ？
Many people watch YouTube videos every day, right?

多くの人は、ネットで検索はグーグルでしょう？
Many people use Google's search engine, right?

わたしで言うと、グーグルドキュメントも結構使っているし。
In my case, I use Google Docs a lot.

コンピューターはマック、携帯はアイフォーンだし。
My computer is a Mac and cell phone is iPhone.

買い物はアマゾンだし。
I do my shopping mostly through Amazon.

日本の政府も、その脅威を感じてGAFAをどうにか抑制しようとする動きもあると思います。
The Japanese government also has concern over GAFA, so they occasionally try to reduce their influence somehow.

ヨーロッパでの罰金もその動きの一部ですよね。
In Europe, fines are one of these trends.

だから今後も罰金やら何やらの、いろんな国の政府からの打撃はあってその都度株価が下がるかもしれません。
Therefore, Google stock prices may be drop occasionally due to those incidents such as fines from governments.

しかし、下がってもまた上がるとは思います。
However, I think it recovers even if the stock price occasionally drops.

バランスシートを見る限り、何か逆境に立たされることがあっても、耐え忍ぶ資金は十分にあります。
As I just check the balance sheet, they have enough financial ability to deal with adverse condition.

株価は一年で見ると、下がっています。(2019年6月13日付)
When we look at the stock prices over the past year, it has declined. (As of 6/13/2019)

5年で見ると、かなり上がっていますが、まあネット環境はかなり変わりましたよね。
For five years, it soared, however, our internet environment changed significantly during the five years.

最大で見ると、10ドルくらいの時に買ってれば、今頃。。。と
言う感じ。

If we look at it for the maximum term, we regret that we
didn't buy it when the stock price was about $10.

今後、5G移行に連れて、大きく伸びるか、各国の政府からの圧
力でどれくらいの打撃があるのか、その辺を考える必要がある
と思いますが、買った株が半分になるようなことはないと思い
ます。

Now along with 5G, we have to think when Google
expands their business significantly, how many countries'
governments will put more pressure on Google. However,
I don't think the stock price will tumble to half of current
stock price.

例えば、政府からの打撃があった時に、30％落ちる、と言うこ
とはありえそうです。

A 30% decrease could be possible if governments attack Google.

でも、それもしばらくすると、回復するように思います。
However, I believe the business would quickly recover.

ある程度調べたら買うか買わないか、もうちょっと安全に
S&P500インデックスファンドにしとくか、と言うところなの
ですが、資金に余力のある方は、遊びココロも取り入れて、
1000万円を５Gになる前に買っておくのも一つだなと思いま
す。
After you analyze the stock for a certain amount of time, you can find any evidence suggesting that the stock price may go up, then you decide whether to buy it or not, or buy low risk S&P 500 Index fund, or if you have extra money, buy ¥10,000,000 (about $100,000) of Google stock before the 5G era starts.

わたしはと言うとグーグル株を1000万円買うのはちょっと怖い
から、500万円かな。。。
In my case, it's too risky to buy ¥10,000,000 (about $100,000) of Google Stock, so maybe I'll just buy ¥5,000,000 (about $50,000).

どちらにしても、10年以上保持の気持ちで買います。
Either way, I will hold onto it for more than 10 years.

以上、「1000万円のグーグル株を買うかどうか」の、2019年
版の結論でした。
That is my conclusion regarding whether or not I should buy ¥10,000,000 (about $100,000) of Google stock (as of summer 2019).

おわりに
Closing

「高校生でも分かる米国株」が終わりました！
This ends "U.S. Stock Even High School Student Can Understand"!

どうでしたか？
How did you like it?

なるべく高校生でも分かるように、簡単に説明をしたつもりです。
I tried to explain U.S. stock investment in a way even high school students can understand.

私は「お金をもっと儲けたい！」とは思っているのですが、実はお金を使うことにはあまり興味がないんです。
I want to make a lot of profit, however, I am actually not so interested in spending money that much.

日本のコンビニでは、数百円で美味しいデザートが買えるし、秋になると焼き芋は美味しいし、サイゼリヤで妹とランチしながらおしゃべりするだけでも楽しいし（ランチ5百円）、そういうことなら、今でも十分できます。
We can buy delicious sweets for only a few hundred yen at convenience stores in Japan. It's fun to chat with my sisters at Saizeriya (lunch set only ¥500), so as long as I have enough money to do that.

去年まではアメリカに進出している日本のメガバンクでフルタイムで働いていました。
I used to work at a Japanese megabank as a full-time employee until last year in USA.

毎日顧客の決算書を分析していましたが、自分が買いたい株の決算書分析をする時間はありませんでした。
I analyzed our borrowers' financial statements, however, I did not have time to analyze the financial statements I was interested in invest in.

毎日が時間との戦いで、期限までにローンを借りたい会社の決算書を分析し、格付し、ローン稟議書を作り、「どうか審査部が私のレポートを承認しますように」と祈る日々でした。
Every day I had to meet deadlines in completing financial statement analyses, ratings, underwritings to lend money, and I would wish, "My God, please let my underwriting be accepted by our examination department by the due date!"

また、顧客の決算書を開く前に、「どうか最終損失を出していませんように。」と祈っていました。
Also, when I received a financial statement from our borrowers, I prayed like, "God, I hope this company does not post a net loss."

最終損失を出していると、お金を貸しても大丈夫な理由を書くのが大変になるからです。
If the company posted a net loss, it's hard for me to explain why it's OK for the bank to lend money to this company.

しかし、今は好きな会社を選んで、期限もなく、誰の承認を得る必要もなく、楽しんで決算書分析ができます。
However, now I can choose my favorite company and analyze the financial conditions with joy without any due date and without anybody's approval.

そんな日々を嬉しく思います。
I am so thankful for that.

それがさらに、これから米国株を買いたい、と思っている人の役に立てるなら、もっと嬉しいです。
I will be even more happy if the information I provide is helpful to others.

期限もない、嫌な上司もいない、なんて素敵な日々！
No due date, no mean bosses, what a wonderful life it is!

「脱サラ、バンザーイ！」
"No more full-time job, yay!!"

最後に、英語の編集と校正をしてくださったエリックさん、ありがとうございました。
And lastly, a special thank you to Eric for his help with editing the English sections and his proofread.

鈴木　花子
Hanako Suzuki

オンラインレッスンの情報(じょうほう)はこちら:
For information regarding my online lessons, visit:
http://www.financewithhanako.com/class/

リソース
Resource Area

ウエブサイトはこちら：
To visit Hanako's website, go to:
http://www.financewithhanako.com

ユーチューブチャンネルはこちら：
To visit Hanako's YouTube channel, go to:
https://www.youtube.com/c/高校生でも分かる米国株

アマゾンで発売中の花子の本はこちら：
Hanako's Book now available on Amazon:
https://www.amazon.com/author/hanakosuzuki

Made in the USA
Monee, IL
03 October 2020